LEO

ANTARES

EPISODE 6

9th CINEBOOK
The 9th Art Publisher

KIM'S VOYAGES

By LEO

KIM KELLER hails from the world of Aldebaran, the only Human colony outside the Solar System. Soon after the arrival of the first colonists on the planet, unexplained accidents resulted in the death of several thousand incoming passengers, leading to the cancellation of all interstellar flights until the cause of the disaster was found. The investigation was to last over a century…

Isolated and few in numbers, the first migrants to Aldebaran eventually built an imperfect society dominated by a retrograde, dictatorial government composed of military personnel and sectarian priests. Kim was born at the end of that period, soon before contact with Earth was re-established.

She came into the world in the small fishing village of Arena Blanca, where she lived peacefully until the age of 13.

There also lived **MARK SORENSEN**, one of Kim's older sister's many suitors.

A disaster shattered the village's peacefulness: a monstrous, gelatinous sea monster engulfed the houses and killed all the inhabitants. Kim, her sister and Mark, away at the time, were the only survivors.

Shortly before the tragedy, a man named **DRISS SHEDIAC** had come to the village to try and warn the people of the approaching danger, but wasn't heeded.

After the destruction of Arena Blanca, Mark decided to leave for the capital. As for Kim and her sister, they were to go to the neighbouring village where their uncle lived. Unsatisfied with that arrangement, Kim decided to accompany Mark without telling him.

Their journey to the capital was eventful, and their relation very tense at first.

During their odyssey, they crossed paths with two characters who would become very important in their lives: **MR PAD**, and above all **ALEXA KOMAROVA**, Driss Shediac's partner.

Mark Sorensen

Driss Shediac

Mr Pad

Alexa Komarova

They eventually arrived at their destination, but not quite the way they'd envisioned it: they had been captured by Church soldiers. While Kim was soon released, Mark remained in prison for three years.

He eventually managed to escape with the help of Mr Pad, and was reunited with the now 18-year-old Kim. She was no longer a scrawny girl but a beautiful young woman, and the two became involved.

That was when Driss and Alexa contacted them to invite them into a small group of carefully selected people with whom they wanted to share a secret – one that they'd been keeping for a long time and that was coveted by the dictatorial authorities: the secret of the Mantris.

The **MANTRIS** was a strange creature that lived in the oceans of Aldebaran. Of gigantic size, it suffered from cyclic mutations that led it to assume different forms. One of those, a particularly dangerous one, was a gelatinous mass weighing several tonnes that absorbed all living organisms it touched by exo-digestion. It was that form that had destroyed Kim's home and killed the villagers. However, most of the time the Mantris was an intelligent being. When a group of scientists had first made contact with it, a strange thing had occurred: the Mantris had offered them a blue capsule that they swallowed without question… As the years passed by, they realised that one of the effects of that capsule was quite beneficial to their organisms – they no longer grew older and had become incredibly healthy. Driss and Alexa were living proof of it, being members of that first group of scientists … as well as the original wave of settlers who had arrived a century before. They looked thirty-something, but at the time they met Kim and Mark they were over a hundred and thirty years old! However, the original small group, who'd consumed the strange creature's blue capsules, had nearly disappeared after a hundred years: a few had died in accidents, others

Alexa among the Gregorias, aquatic creatures from Aldebaran. Next page: the lums of Betelgeuse.

had committed suicide, and yet others had been killed inside the government's prisons. The authorities, eager to get their hands on that miraculous blue capsule and its amazing properties, didn't hesitate to torture members of the group to achieve their goal. Driss and Alexa were the last survivors.

So they decided to reveal their secret to a few chosen people who would go with them to their next visit to the Mantris, in the hope that it would give its capsule to the newcomers – thus forming a new 'Mantris group'.

At first, their plan failed. They were arrested by the authorities, who forced them to lead them to the meeting place. There, by the colossal, static shape the strange creature had assumed, the members of the government attempted to take the place of the original group and seize the miraculous capsules for themselves. But they forgot that the Mantris was intelligent and only gave its bounty to those it believed to be persons of quality. The trick failed: the Mantris killed the dictatorial authorities and then soon afterwards provided the people chosen by Driss and Alexa with its capsules. A new Mantris group was born, which included Kim, Mark and – almost by accident – the outrageous Mr Pad.

Almost at the exact same time, contact was re-established with Earth as a ship carrying thousands of new colonists arrived. The dictatorship was ended and Aldebaran entered a period of peace and progress. An institute dedicated to the study of that extraordinary marine creature, the Mantris, was created, in the hope of learning how to communicate with it.

Kim and Mark left for Earth, as seeing the home world was the young woman's old dream. There they stayed for a few years, with Kim studying biology and Mark spaceship piloting.

When Kim returned to Aldebaran, she was 24. Mark had decided to remain on Earth, leaving a hiatus in their relationship. To Kim's surprise, she was immediately offered a dangerous but fascinating mission: to go to Betelgeuse 4 to investigate what had happened to the passengers of the *Konstantin Tsiolkowsky*. Having reached its destination, the colony ship had established orbit. Several crew members had descended to the surface and then communications had been severed; no signs of life had arrived in six years. A small ship was therefore going to be sent there, with two members of the Space Corps. Kim would accompany them as a representative of the Mantris Group.

As it happened, the institute in charge of studying the Mantris had noticed that it had directed the antennae it regularly built in the sea towards the star Betelgeuse – and had done so many times. The presence of another Mantris on Betelgeuse 4 was therefore suspected.

One of the manifestations of the Mantris.

That mission to Betelgeuse was to have a profound impact on Kim's existence. She met not one but two Mantrisses, with whom she managed to communicate. They conveyed to her the fact that they were the cause of the Human ships' computer malfunctions. By cutting off all communications, they wanted to prevent Humans from settling on the planet, in order to protect an endemic, sentient species living there – the lums.

But Kim was also affected by a serious abdominal injury. She came close to death and owed her survival purely to the improved healing abilities bestowed by the Mantris's capsules.

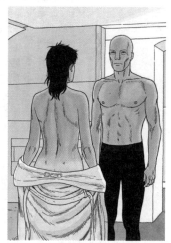

Kim and Sven

Mark and Pad's assistance. Afterwards, though, Alexa and Mark were arrested and sentenced to extensive prison time, while Mr Pad escaped and went to ground on Betelgeuse.

It was to rehabilitate them that Kim agreed – reluctantly – to join the Antares mission. Elijah Thornton, the project leader, was willing to invite Alexa, Pad and Mark to join the expedition, which according to an obscure law would cause their sentences to be commuted. The plan was for Kim to be kept far from any dangerous situation as a simple consultant, allowing her to bring along her daughter – especially as Mai Lan had also signed up and could help her take care of the child.

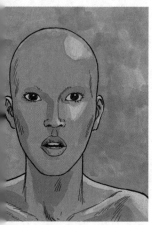

Mai Lan

On Betelgeuse Kim met **MAI LAN**, a young girl who, over the years, became a surrogate little sister.

It was also on that planet that Kim had an astonishing encounter: **SVEN**, an alien belonging to a race more advanced than Humans and native to the same planet as the Mantrisses. Fascinated by Kim, he even fell in love with her. Eventually he engineered a meeting and seduced her, leading to a sexual encounter … and a most improbable result: Kim became pregnant and gave birth to a little **LYNN**.

Meanwhile, Alexa was left without any news from Kim, whose ship too had broken down because of the Mantrisses. The 140-year-old woman decided to steal a ship and go and look for her, with

But they were all the victims of the inevitable hazards of an endeavour as ambitious as it was uncertain. Several accidents forced Kim into very dangerous adventures. Worst of all, little Lynn was taken by an unknown beam of light, sending Kim on an even more perilous trek to the neighbouring planet to look for her.

PREVIOUSLY

Kim's daughter Lynn has appeared for the first time since her sudden vanishing. But Kim is bitterly disappointed to find out that it's only a holographic image. Desperate, she receives emotional support from her companions, including Alexa. Sven, Lynn's alien father, witnesses the terrible scene but isn't authorised to intervene. Tension among the group rises a notch when a mysterious sphere appears and then promptly disappears into Kim's shuttle. Then another shuttle, completely identical to theirs, materialises before their eyes. Intent on finding out what is going on, they decide to climb aboard. First among them is Jedediah, convinced he is the 'chosen one' who will establish first contact with the alien civilisation…

I've long wanted to thank Philippe Ravon. Through Studio Dargaud, he completed, corrected or improved many of my covers, always with subtle and delicate talent. Thank you very much, Philippe!

Unlike my first books, this one was entirely coloured by computer. To learn how to do that, I received the invaluable help of Camille Aubry. Patiently and efficiently, she taught me the basics of digital colourisation. Thank you, Camille!

I am very fortunate to have a nephew, Caetano Brasil, who is a genius graphic designer. He's always followed my work, and he was the one who introduced me to the advantages of digital creation and guided me through my choices. Via our frequent exchanges, he helps me to improve. And he's also the one I call, all the way in his distant Brazil, when I'm stuck in the middle of a piece because of some apparently insoluble problem caused by the complicated programs that rule over digital art. *Obrigado*, Caetano!

Leo

Original title: Episode 6
Original edition: © Dargaud Paris, 2015 by LEO
www.dargaud.com
All rights reserved
English translation: © 2015 Cinebook Ltd
Translator: Jerome Saincantin
Lettering and text layout: Design Amorandi
Printed in Spain by EGEDSA
This edition first published in Great Britain in 2015 by
Cinebook Ltd
56 Beech Avenue
Canterbury, Kent
CT4 7TA
www.cinebook.com
A CIP catalogue record for this book
is available from the British Library
ISBN 978-1-84918-258-4

9th CINEBOOK
The 9th Art Publisher

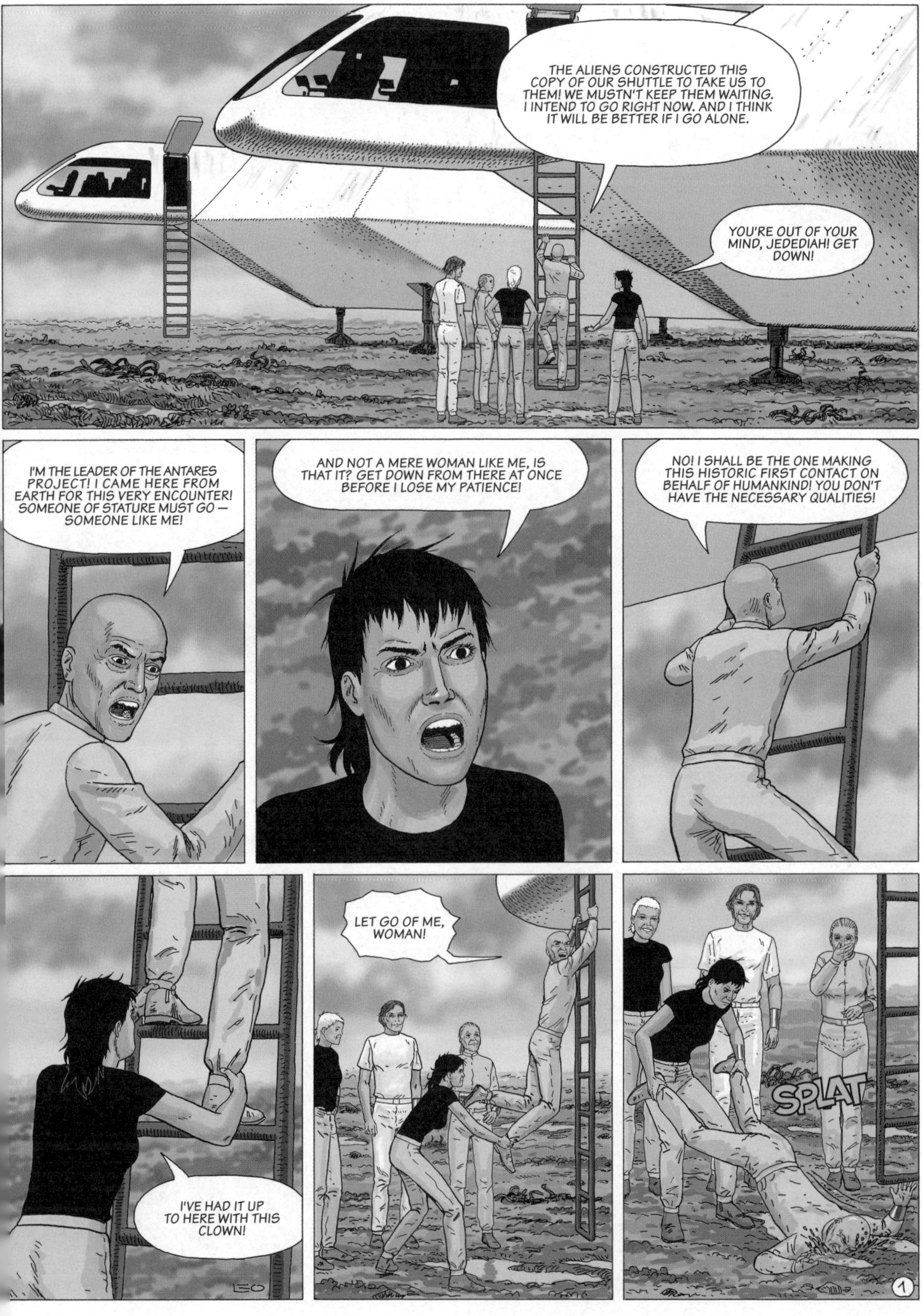

THE ALIENS CONSTRUCTED THIS COPY OF OUR SHUTTLE TO TAKE US TO THEM! WE MUSTN'T KEEP THEM WAITING. I INTEND TO GO RIGHT NOW. AND I THINK IT WILL BE BETTER IF I GO ALONE.
YOU'RE OUT OF YOUR MIND, JEDEDIAH! GET DOWN!
I'M THE LEADER OF THE ANTARES PROJECT! I CAME HERE FROM EARTH FOR THIS VERY ENCOUNTER! SOMEONE OF STATURE MUST GO — SOMEONE LIKE ME!
AND NOT A MERE WOMAN LIKE ME, IS THAT IT? GET DOWN FROM THERE AT ONCE BEFORE I LOSE MY PATIENCE!
NO! I SHALL BE THE ONE MAKING THIS HISTORIC FIRST CONTACT ON BEHALF OF HUMANKIND! YOU DON'T HAVE THE NECESSARY QUALITIES!
I'VE HAD IT UP TO HERE WITH THIS CLOWN!
LEO
LET GO OF ME, WOMAN!
SPLAT
1

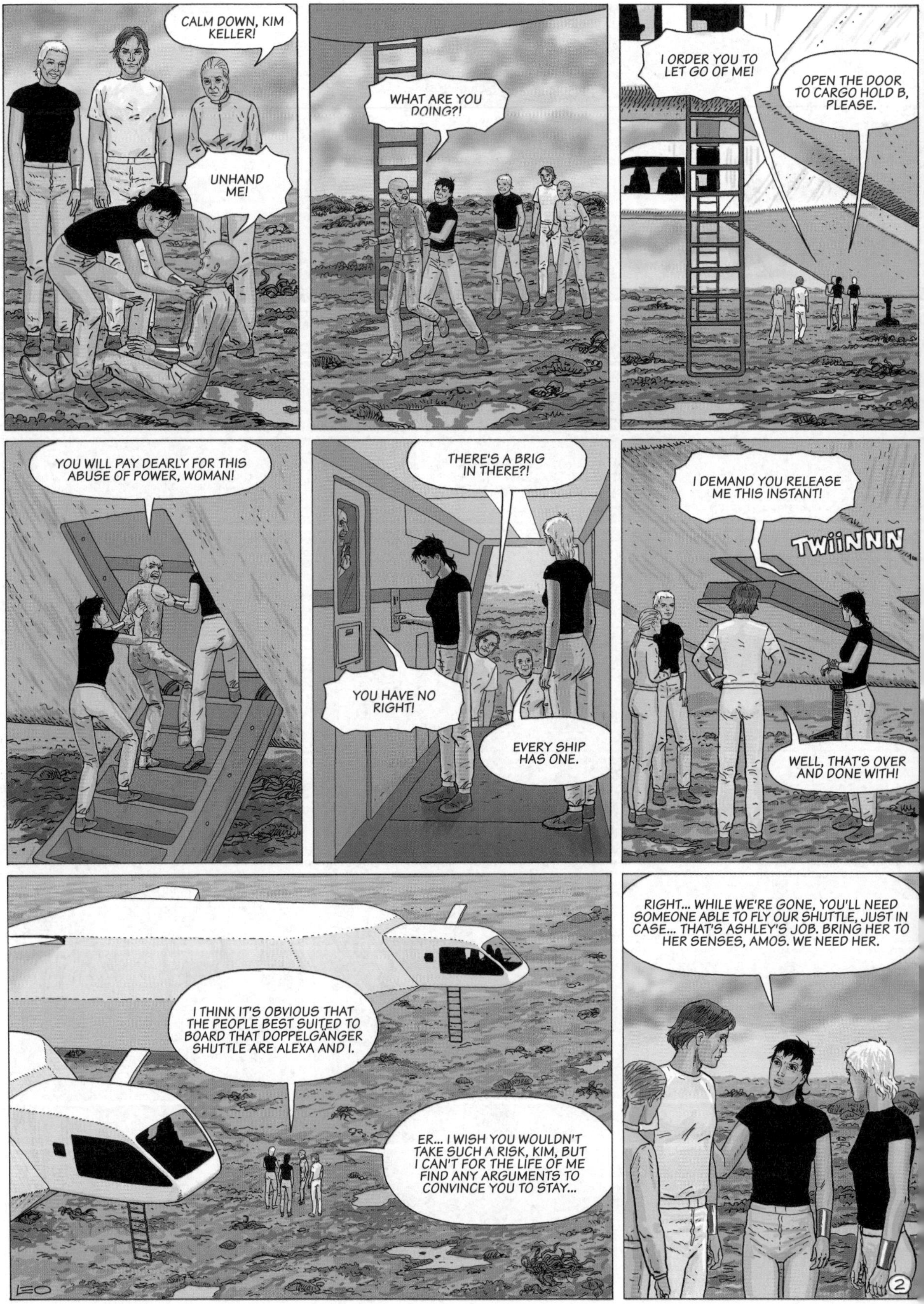
CALM DOWN, KIM KELLER!
UNHAND ME!
WHAT ARE YOU DOING?!
I ORDER YOU TO LET GO OF ME!
OPEN THE DOOR TO CARGO HOLD B, PLEASE.
YOU WILL PAY DEARLY FOR THIS ABUSE OF POWER, WOMAN!
THERE'S A BRIG IN THERE?!
YOU HAVE NO RIGHT!
EVERY SHIP HAS ONE.
I DEMAND YOU RELEASE ME THIS INSTANT!
TWIINNN
WELL, THAT'S OVER AND DONE WITH!
I THINK IT'S OBVIOUS THAT THE PEOPLE BEST SUITED TO BOARD THAT DOPPELGÄNGER SHUTTLE ARE ALEXA AND I.
ER... I WISH YOU WOULDN'T TAKE SUCH A RISK, KIM, BUT I CAN'T FOR THE LIFE OF ME FIND ANY ARGUMENTS TO CONVINCE YOU TO STAY...
LEO
RIGHT... WHILE WE'RE GONE, YOU'LL NEED SOMEONE ABLE TO FLY OUR SHUTTLE, JUST IN CASE... THAT'S ASHLEY'S JOB. BRING HER TO HER SENSES, AMOS. WE NEED HER.
2

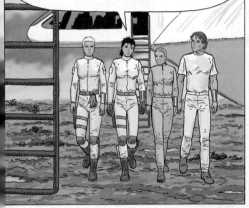

I DON'T KNOW EXACTLY WHAT WILL HAPPEN, BUT AFTER THIS SECOND SHUTTLE LEAVES — IF IT LEAVES — DON'T WAIT FOR US MORE THAN THREE DAYS BEFORE RETURNING TO BASE. THAT'S THE LIMIT DICTATED BY YOUR FOOD AND WATER RESERVES. ASHLEY CAN FLY THE SHUTTLE ALONE.

WISH US LUCK — WE'RE GOING TO NEED IT!

WELL... NO POINT IN WASTING TIME.

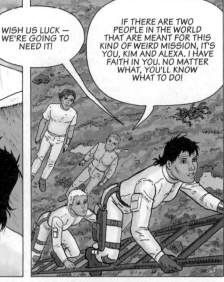

IF THERE ARE TWO PEOPLE IN THE WORLD THAT ARE MEANT FOR THIS KIND OF WEIRD MISSION, IT'S YOU, KIM AND ALEXA. I HAVE FAITH IN YOU. NO MATTER WHAT, YOU'LL KNOW WHAT TO DO!

I WISH I WAS AS CERTAIN AS YOU, SURIA, BUT THE TRUTH IS I'M SCARED TO DEATH! MY HANDS ARE SHAKING!

SSSST

!

GOOD LORD! IT'S UNBELIEVABLE! THAT THING DISAPPEARED INSTANTLY!

IT HAD TO BE EXPECTED... THEY'VE BEEN TAKEN SOMEWHERE. THE WORST THING WOULD HAVE BEEN FOR NOTHING TO HAPPEN.

MAYBE, BUT I'M STILL WORRIED, DOCTOR... I'M BEGINNING TO DOUBT OUR DECISION TO ENTER THAT PHANTOM SHUTTLE!

IT'S WHAT WE HAD TO DO, SURIA...

I'LL GO AND SPEAK TO ASHLEY SCOTT... TRY AND MAKE HER GET A GRIP ON HERSELF.

WOULD YOU LIKE ME TO COME WITH YOU?

NO, SURIA. THIS WILL BE A PATIENT–DOCTOR CONVERSATION, YOU SEE...

ASHLEY, YOU HAVE TO COME.

LEAVE ME ALONE, DOCTOR. I WILL NOT LEAVE MY CABIN UNTIL WE'RE OFF THIS BLASTED PLANET.

AH! WHAT ARE YOU... ?!

HOW DARE YOU?!...

WE NEED YOU, ASHLEY! WHY DON'T YOU COME TO YOUR SENSES! YOU'RE AN OFFICER OF THE UN SPACE CORPS. PULL YOURSELF TOGETHER!

KIM AND ALEXA HAVE DISAPPEARED ABOARD A REPLICA OF OUR SHUTTLE THAT MATERIALISED AS IF BY MAGIC. IT'S JUST YOU, SURIA AND ME NOW — NOT COUNTING THAT LUNATIC JEDEDIAH!

DISAPPEARED?! DISAPPEARED HOW?!

I DON'T KNOW! THE SHUTTLE VANISHED IN A SPLIT SECOND, WITH THE TWO OF THEM INSIDE! SO STOP BEHAVING LIKE A HYSTERICAL TEENAGER AND COME. WE NEED TO BE READY TO ASSIST KIM AND ALEXA IF THEY NEED US!

④

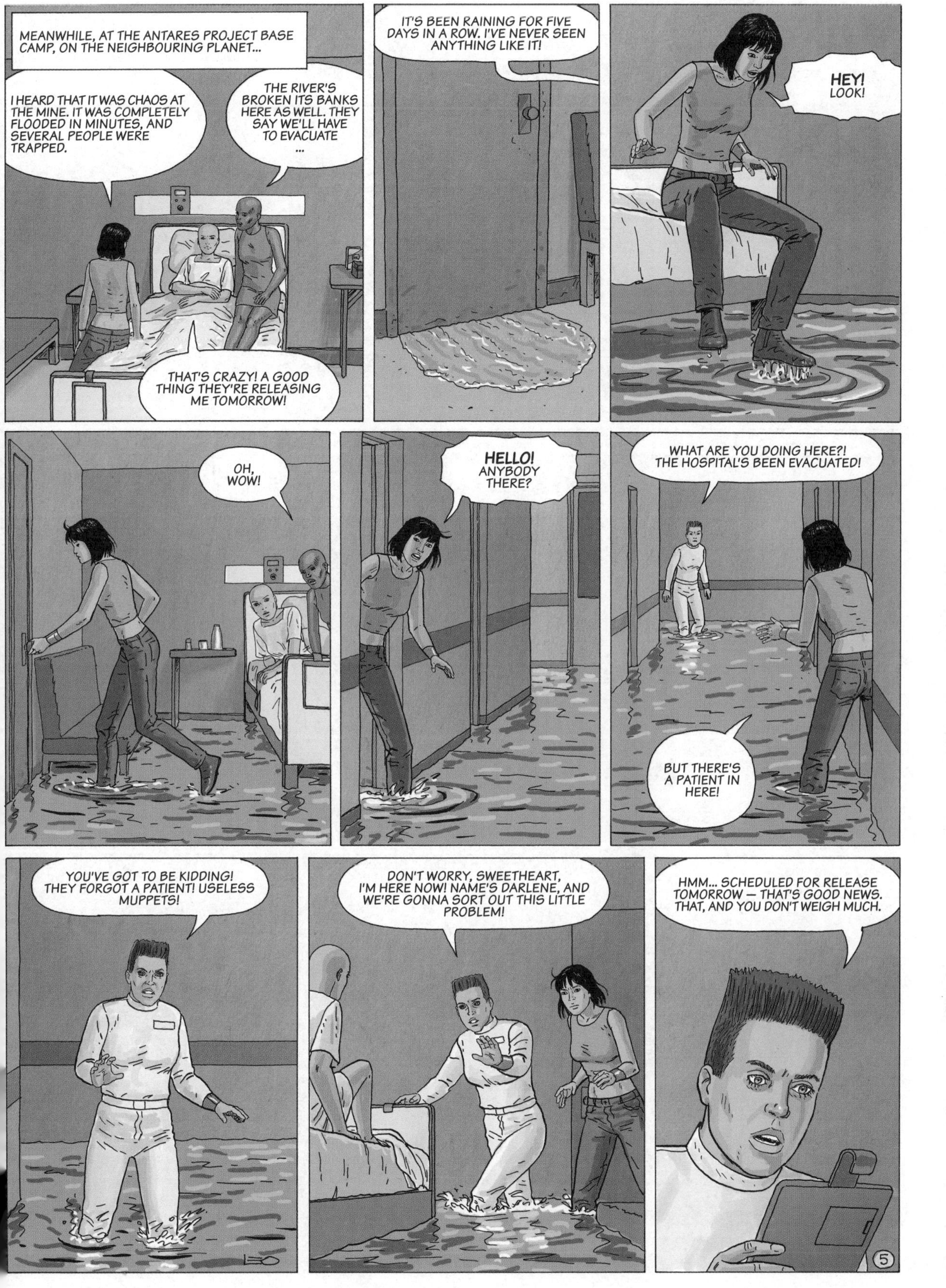
MEANWHILE, AT THE ANTARES PROJECT BASE CAMP, ON THE NEIGHBOURING PLANET...
I HEARD THAT IT WAS CHAOS AT THE MINE. IT WAS COMPLETELY FLOODED IN MINUTES, AND SEVERAL PEOPLE WERE TRAPPED.
THE RIVER'S BROKEN ITS BANKS HERE AS WELL. THEY SAY WE'LL HAVE TO EVACUATE ...
THAT'S CRAZY! A GOOD THING THEY'RE RELEASING ME TOMORROW!
IT'S BEEN RAINING FOR FIVE DAYS IN A ROW. I'VE NEVER SEEN ANYTHING LIKE IT!
HEY! LOOK!
OH, WOW!
HELLO! ANYBODY THERE?
WHAT ARE YOU DOING HERE?! THE HOSPITAL'S BEEN EVACUATED!
BUT THERE'S A PATIENT IN HERE!
YOU'VE GOT TO BE KIDDING! THEY FORGOT A PATIENT! USELESS MUPPETS!
DON'T WORRY, SWEETHEART, I'M HERE NOW! NAME'S DARLENE, AND WE'RE GONNA SORT OUT THIS LITTLE PROBLEM!
HMM... SCHEDULED FOR RELEASE TOMORROW — THAT'S GOOD NEWS. THAT, AND YOU DON'T WEIGH MUCH.
LEO
5

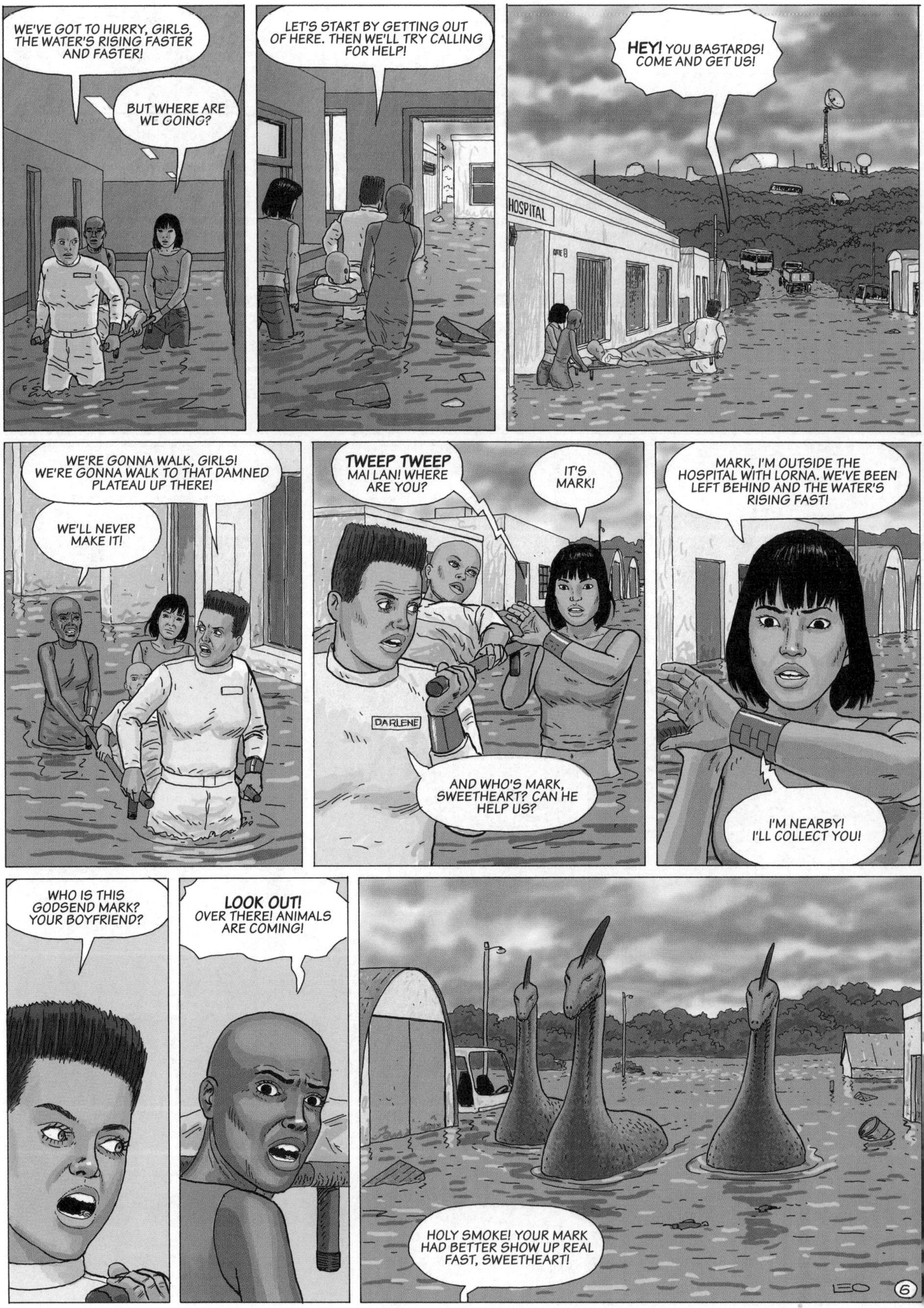
WE'VE GOT TO HURRY, GIRLS, THE WATER'S RISING FASTER AND FASTER!
BUT WHERE ARE WE GOING?
LET'S START BY GETTING OUT OF HERE. THEN WE'LL TRY CALLING FOR HELP!
HEY! YOU BASTARDS! COME AND GET US!
HOSPITAL
WE'RE GONNA WALK, GIRLS! WE'RE GONNA WALK TO THAT DAMNED PLATEAU UP THERE!
WE'LL NEVER MAKE IT!
TWEEP TWEEP MAI LAN! WHERE ARE YOU?
IT'S MARK!
DARLENE
AND WHO'S MARK, SWEETHEART? CAN HE HELP US?
MARK, I'M OUTSIDE THE HOSPITAL WITH LORNA. WE'VE BEEN LEFT BEHIND AND THE WATER'S RISING FAST!
I'M NEARBY! I'LL COLLECT YOU!
WHO IS THIS GODSEND MARK? YOUR BOYFRIEND?
LOOK OUT! OVER THERE! ANIMALS ARE COMING!
HOLY SMOKE! YOUR MARK HAD BETTER SHOW UP REAL FAST, SWEETHEART!
LEO
6

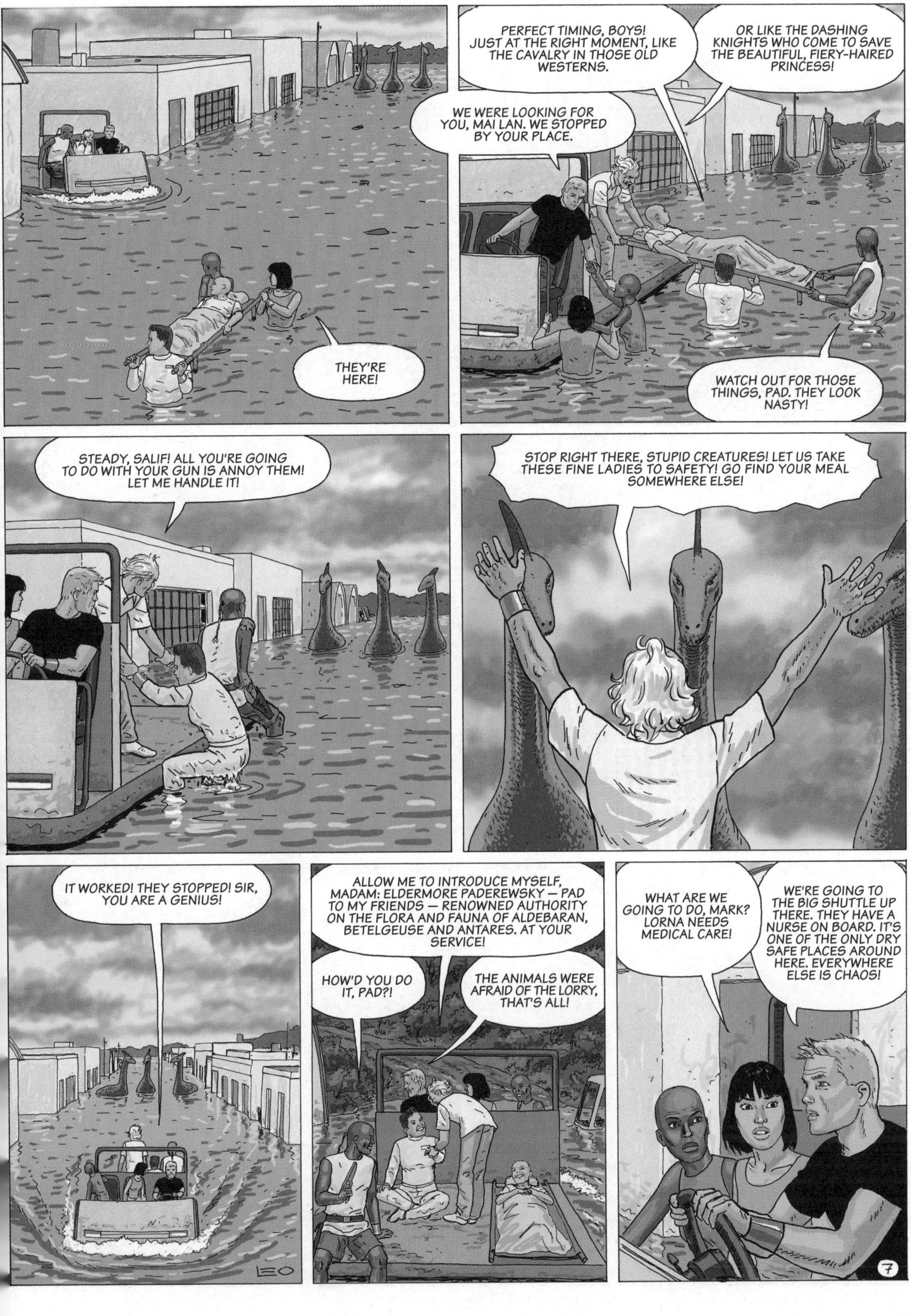
THEY'RE HERE!
PERFECT TIMING, BOYS! JUST AT THE RIGHT MOMENT, LIKE THE CAVALRY IN THOSE OLD WESTERNS.
OR LIKE THE DASHING KNIGHTS WHO COME TO SAVE THE BEAUTIFUL, FIERY-HAIRED PRINCESS!
WE WERE LOOKING FOR YOU, MAI LAN. WE STOPPED BY YOUR PLACE.
WATCH OUT FOR THOSE THINGS, PAD. THEY LOOK NASTY!
STEADY, SALIF! ALL YOU'RE GOING TO DO WITH YOUR GUN IS ANNOY THEM! LET ME HANDLE IT!
STOP RIGHT THERE, STUPID CREATURES! LET US TAKE THESE FINE LADIES TO SAFETY! GO FIND YOUR MEAL SOMEWHERE ELSE!
IT WORKED! THEY STOPPED! SIR, YOU ARE A GENIUS!
LEO
ALLOW ME TO INTRODUCE MYSELF, MADAM: ELDERMORE PADEREWSKY — PAD TO MY FRIENDS — RENOWNED AUTHORITY ON THE FLORA AND FAUNA OF ALDEBARAN, BETELGEUSE AND ANTARES. AT YOUR SERVICE!
HOW'D YOU DO IT, PAD?!
THE ANIMALS WERE AFRAID OF THE LORRY, THAT'S ALL!
WHAT ARE WE GOING TO DO, MARK? LORNA NEEDS MEDICAL CARE!
WE'RE GOING TO THE BIG SHUTTLE UP THERE. THEY HAVE A NURSE ON BOARD. IT'S ONE OF THE ONLY DRY SAFE PLACES AROUND HERE. EVERYWHERE ELSE IS CHAOS!
7

WE HAVE TO DO SOMETHING! WE CAN'T JUST STAY HERE TWIDDLING OUR THUMBS!

DO WHAT, THOUGH? WHAT CAN WE DO?

I SEE NO OTHER OPTION THAN TO WAIT, DOCTOR...

THE SMALL MYSTERY SHIP! IT'S STILL THERE, A SHORT HOP FROM HERE. ITS OCCUPANTS ARE PROBABLY THE ONES CONTROLLING THE SPHERE. WE COULD GO TO THEM, TRY TO COMMUNICATE WITH THEM, FIND OUT WHAT'S GOING ON WITH KIM AND ALEXA...

BUT WE HAVE NO TRANSPORTATION. ARE YOU PLANNING TO WALK THERE?!

THE HOIST! WE HAVE THE HOIST!

THERE ARE TOO FEW OF US. REGULATIONS STATE THAT A GROUP OF LESS THAN FIVE MUSTN'T SPLIT UP.

SCREW REGULATIONS, ASHLEY! THIS IS AN EMERGENCY SITUATION!

THE TWO OF US COULD GO, ASHLEY, AND...

NO! I CAN'T STAY HERE ALONE! WITH JEDEDIAH TOO! IF ANYTHING HAPPENED TO YOU, I WOULDN'T BE ABLE TO FLY THE SHUTTLE. ASHLEY HAS TO STAY HERE!

THEN COME WITH ME, SURIA.

BUT YOU'VE NEVER CONTROLLED A HOIST, DOCTOR!

THEN YOU'LL TEACH ME! ASHLEY, I CAN CONTROL A SURGERY ROBOT; I CAN HANDLE SOME STUPID HOIST!

DOCTOR, DOCTOR... YOU'RE A LITTLE ON EDGE! I THINK YOUR ATTRACTION TOWARDS OUR LOVELY COMMANDER KIM KELLER IS CLOUDING YOUR JUDGEMENT.

ON THE CONTRARY, SURIA, IT'S MAKING ME MORE CLEAR-HEADED AND MORE DETERMINED. IF YOU WON'T COME WITH ME, I'LL GO ALONE.

FLYING THIS THING IS CHILD'S PLAY! AND STOP CRANING YOUR NECK AROUND LIKE THAT, SURIA. THERE AREN'T MONSTERS EVERY TEN METRES, EVEN HERE...

DOCTOR, IF I MANAGED TO REACH SUCH A VENERABLE AGE IT'S BECAUSE I'VE ALWAYS BEEN CAREFUL!

WHAT SHOULD WE DO? MOVE?

NO, WE JUST HAVE TO OPACIFY THE VIEW PORTS. THEY KNOW WE'RE HERE, ANYWAY.

THERE IT IS! IT'S PRETTY SMALL, ISN'T IT?!

THERE MUST BE A LARGER MOTHER SHIP IN ORBIT... ANYWAY, I STILL HAVE NO IDEA WHAT YOU INTEND TO DO NOW. WHAT'S YOUR PLAN?

I'M GOING TO IMPROVISE, SURIA. I WANT TO SHOW THEM THAT WE KNOW THEY'RE HERE. I WANT TO PROVOKE A REACTION FROM THEM.

I'M HAVING GOOSEBUMPS, DOCTOR! TO KNOW THAT WE'RE IN THE PRESENCE OF AN ALIEN SHIP! AND THAT INSIDE IT ARE BEINGS FROM ANOTHER PLANET, LOOKING AT US!

I'M PRETTY OVERWHELMED TOO, SURIA...

IT'S FLOATING, LIKE THE SPHERE.

THERE ARE NO DOORS, NO VIEW PORTS. THEY MUST BE WATCHING US THROUGH CAMERAS.

HEY! COME AND TALK TO US! THERE'S NO POINT IN STAYING INSIDE JUST OBSERVING US. COME AND TELL US WHAT YOU DID WITH OUR TEAMMATES!

ONE OF THEM IS KIM KELLER, OUR CAPTAIN. SHE'S THE LOVE OF MY LIFE. I HAVE TO KNOW WHAT'S HAPPENING TO HER RIGHT NOW!

AND I HOPE YOU'LL RETURN HER LITTLE GIRL. SHE DOESN'T DESERVE TO SUFFER SO MUCH. SHE'S A WONDERFUL WOMAN. GIVER HER BACK HER DAUGHTER!

I DON'T KNOW IF THERE'S ANY POINT IN TALKING TO THEM LIKE THIS... BUT I NEEDED TO SAY WHAT I SAID. CAN YOU UNDERSTAND THAT, SURIA?

YES, AMOS BLUM, I UNDERSTAND...

LET'S GO BACK, SURIA. OUR PRESENCE HERE IS POINTLESS. IF THEY WANT TO TALK TO US, THEY KNOW WHERE TO FIND US...

WHAT DID HE SAY? DID YOU UNDERSTAND HIM?

YES, ELTVEN. I'M FLUENT IN THEIR LANGUAGE. THEY THINK WE'RE RESPONSIBLE FOR THE SPHERE'S ACTIONS, AND THEY'RE AFRAID FOR THE TWO WOMEN WHO VANISHED.

HE SEEMED QUITE EMOTIONAL. I BELIEVE HE, TOO, IS ATTRACTED TO THAT WOMAN... THE SAME AS YOU?

I TOLD YOU SHE'S A FASCINATING WOMAN.

BACK AT BASE CAMP...

YOU CAN'T STAY HERE! GET BACK! GET BACK!

WE'RE BRINGING IN AN INVALID THAT WAS LEFT BEHIND AT THE HOSPITAL. MOVE THE DAMNED BARRIER, YOU FOOL!

GASOLINE.

10

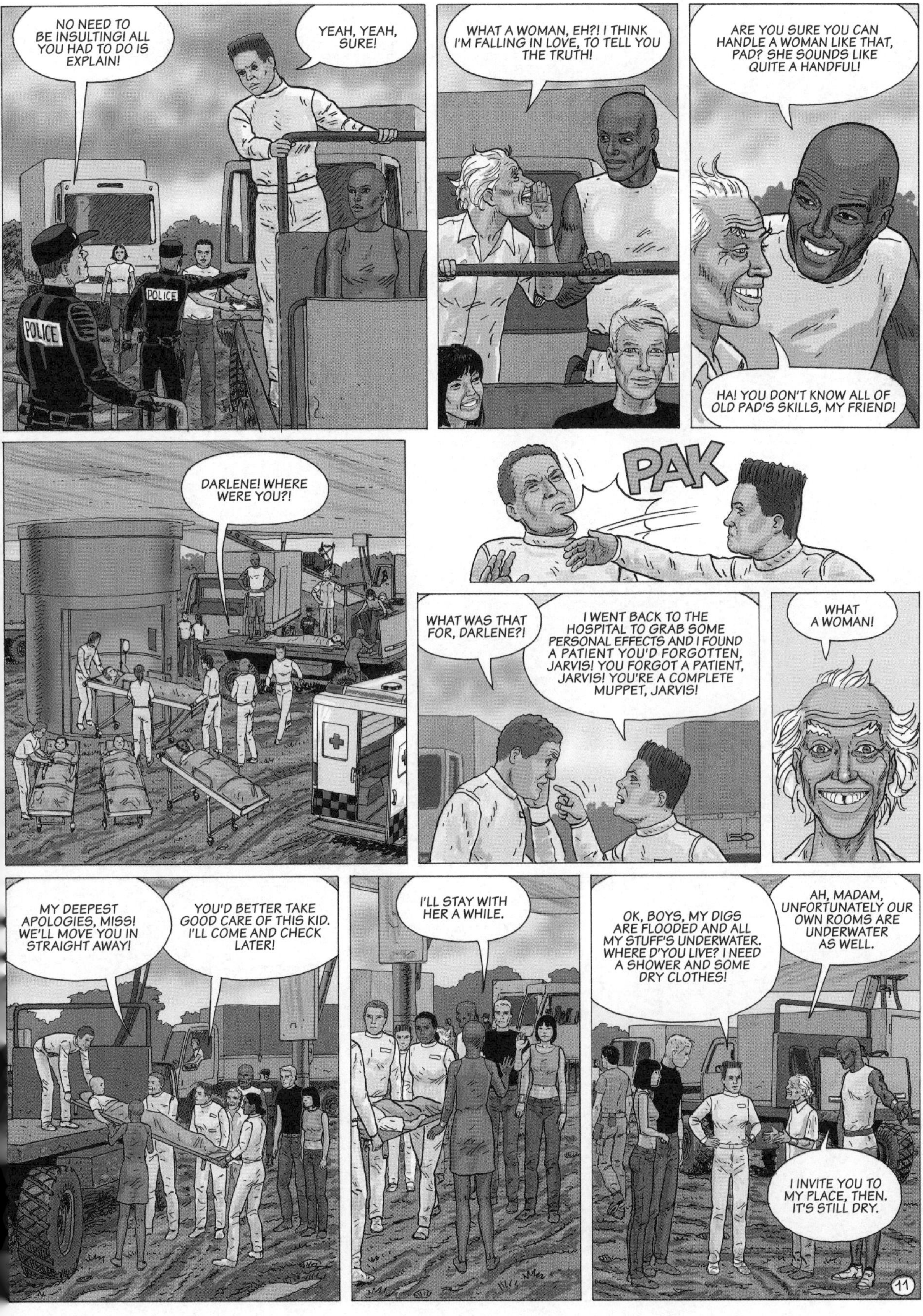
NO NEED TO BE INSULTING! ALL YOU HAD TO DO IS EXPLAIN!
YEAH, YEAH, SURE!
POLICE
POLICE
WHAT A WOMAN, EH?! I THINK I'M FALLING IN LOVE, TO TELL YOU THE TRUTH!
ARE YOU SURE YOU CAN HANDLE A WOMAN LIKE THAT, PAD? SHE SOUNDS LIKE QUITE A HANDFUL!
HA! YOU DON'T KNOW ALL OF OLD PAD'S SKILLS, MY FRIEND!
DARLENE! WHERE WERE YOU?!
PAK
WHAT WAS THAT FOR, DARLENE?!
I WENT BACK TO THE HOSPITAL TO GRAB SOME PERSONAL EFFECTS AND I FOUND A PATIENT YOU'D FORGOTTEN, JARVIS! YOU FORGOT A PATIENT, JARVIS! YOU'RE A COMPLETE MUPPET, JARVIS!
WHAT A WOMAN!
MY DEEPEST APOLOGIES, MISS! WE'LL MOVE YOU IN STRAIGHT AWAY!
YOU'D BETTER TAKE GOOD CARE OF THIS KID. I'LL COME AND CHECK LATER!
I'LL STAY WITH HER A WHILE.
OK, BOYS, MY DIGS ARE FLOODED AND ALL MY STUFF'S UNDERWATER. WHERE D'YOU LIVE? I NEED A SHOWER AND SOME DRY CLOTHES!
AH, MADAM, UNFORTUNATELY OUR OWN ROOMS ARE UNDERWATER AS WELL.
I INVITE YOU TO MY PLACE, THEN. IT'S STILL DRY.
11

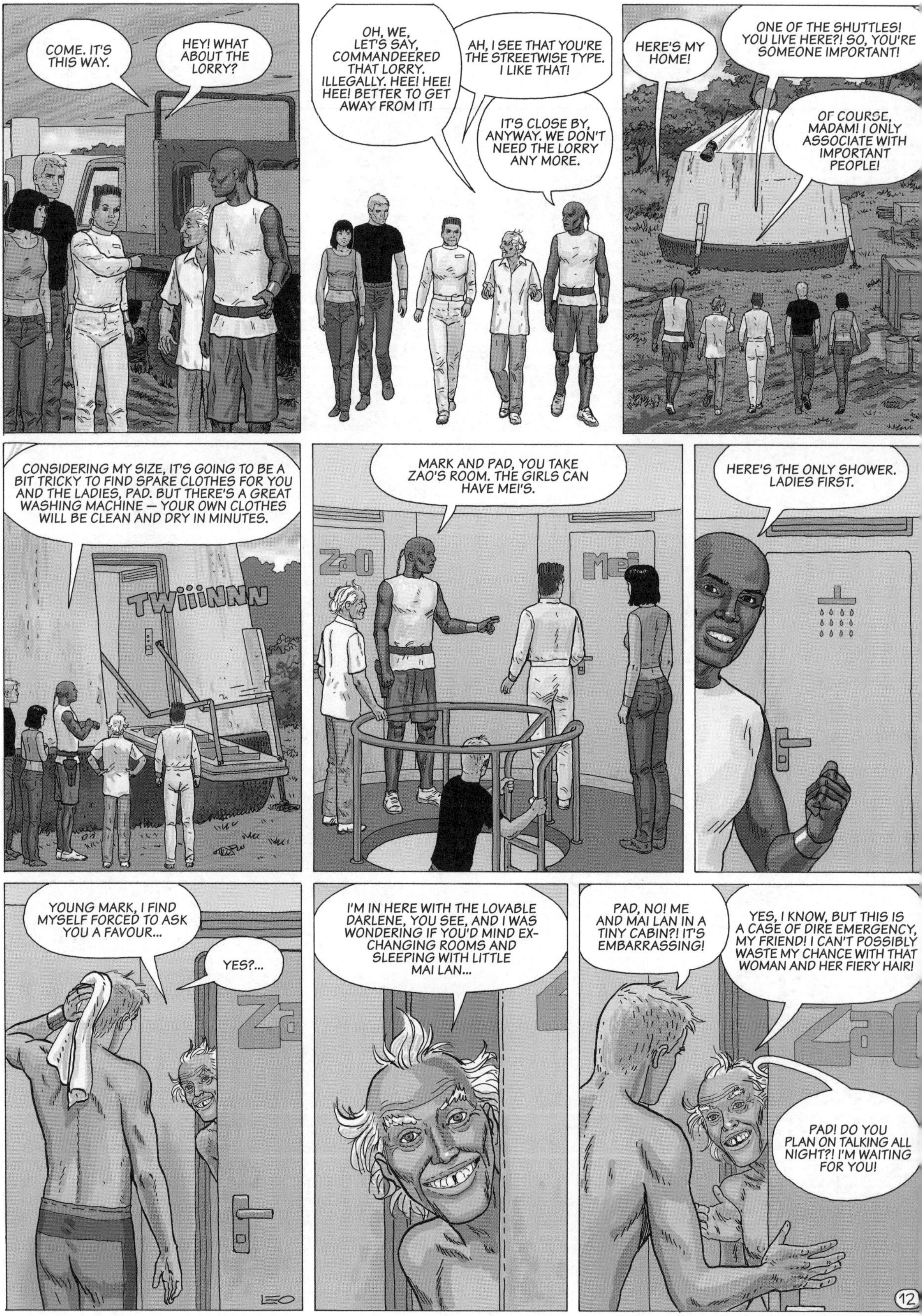
COME. IT'S THIS WAY.
HEY! WHAT ABOUT THE LORRY?
OH, WE, LET'S SAY, COMMANDEERED THAT LORRY. ILLEGALLY. HEE! HEE! HEE! BETTER TO GET AWAY FROM IT!
AH, I SEE THAT YOU'RE THE STREETWISE TYPE. I LIKE THAT!
IT'S CLOSE BY, ANYWAY. WE DON'T NEED THE LORRY ANY MORE.
HERE'S MY HOME!
ONE OF THE SHUTTLES! YOU LIVE HERE?! SO, YOU'RE SOMEONE IMPORTANT!
OF COURSE, MADAM! I ONLY ASSOCIATE WITH IMPORTANT PEOPLE!
CONSIDERING MY SIZE, IT'S GOING TO BE A BIT TRICKY TO FIND SPARE CLOTHES FOR YOU AND THE LADIES, PAD. BUT THERE'S A GREAT WASHING MACHINE — YOUR OWN CLOTHES WILL BE CLEAN AND DRY IN MINUTES.
TWIIINNN
MARK AND PAD, YOU TAKE ZAO'S ROOM. THE GIRLS CAN HAVE MEI'S.
ZaO
Mei
HERE'S THE ONLY SHOWER. LADIES FIRST.
YOUNG MARK, I FIND MYSELF FORCED TO ASK YOU A FAVOUR...
YES?...
I'M IN HERE WITH THE LOVABLE DARLENE, YOU SEE, AND I WAS WONDERING IF YOU'D MIND EX-CHANGING ROOMS AND SLEEPING WITH LITTLE MAI LAN...
PAD, NO! ME AND MAI LAN IN A TINY CABIN?! IT'S EMBARRASSING!
YES, I KNOW, BUT THIS IS A CASE OF DIRE EMERGENCY, MY FRIEND! I CAN'T POSSIBLY WASTE MY CHANCE WITH THAT WOMAN AND HER FIERY HAIR!
PAD! DO YOU PLAN ON TALKING ALL NIGHT?! I'M WAITING FOR YOU!
LEO
12

I'VE ALREADY SPOKEN TO MAI LAN. SHE SAID THERE WAS NO PROBLEM AS FAR AS SHE WAS CONCERNED.

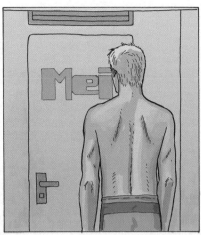

KNOCK KNOCK

COME IN, MARK...

ER... DID PAD SPEAK TO YOU?

YES...

OLD PAD PLAYED A WICKED TRICK ON US... BOTH OF US TOGETHER IN THIS MINUSCULE CABIN, AND YOU WEARING ONLY A TEENSY BLANKET...

IT WASN'T MY IDEA, MARK. PAD'S THE ONE WHO ORGANISED THIS, AND MY CLOTHES ARE STILL IN THE WASH...

TAKE IT EASY, MAI LAN, I'M NOT ACCUSING YOU OF ANYTHING. YOU KNOW... IN THE END, MAYBE IT WAS FATE THAT PLAYED A TRICK ON US, BECAUSE I THINK...

...I DON'T HAVE THE STRENGTH TO HOLD BACK ANY MORE, MAI LAN. I WANT YOU. I WANT YOU LIKE CRAZY!

13

OH, LORD! WHAT I WOULDN'T GIVE TO BE BACK HOME ON EARTH, WATCHING SOME OLD FILM AND EATING CHOCOLATE ICE CREAM...

CHOCOLATE ICE CREAM?! IT'D BE A GLASS OF GOOD FRENCH WINE FOR ME!

I OWE YOU AN APOLOGY FOR MY EARLIER BEHAVIOUR. I'M SORRY. I CRACKED.

UNDERSTANDABLE, CONSIDERING WHAT YOU WENT THROUGH, COMMANDER SCOTT ...

BACK ON EARTH, WHEN I AGREED TO PARTICIPATE IN THE ANTARES PROJECT, I COULD NEVER HAVE IMAGINED HAVING ALL THESE ABSURD ADVENTURES! IT'S HELL ON THE NERVES!

PUT YOURSELF IN KIM'S SHOES, ASHLEY. WHAT SHE WENT THROUGH ON ALDEBARAN, THEN BETELGEUSE, AND NOW HERE!...

IT'S TRUE! I DON'T KNOW HOW SHE CAN HANDLE IT!

SHE'S A REMARKABLE WOMAN. A FORCE OF NATURE!

AND BEAUTIFUL TO BOOT! NO WONDER I ENDED UP FALLING IN LOVE WITH HER, EH?

LOVING A WOMAN LIKE KIM ISN'T EASY, DOCTOR...

I KNOW, SURIA. BUT SHE'S WELL WORTH THE RISK!...

5 HOURS AND 47 MINUTES EARLIER...

WELL... NO POINT IN WASTING TIME.

WISH US LUCK — WE'RE GOING TO NEED IT!

IF THERE ARE TWO PEOPLE IN THE WORLD THAT ARE MEANT FOR THIS KIND OF WEIRD MISSION, IT'S YOU, KIM AND ALEXA. I HAVE FAITH IN YOU. NO MATTER WHAT, YOU'LL KNOW WHAT TO DO!

I WISH I WAS AS CERTAIN AS YOU, SURIA, BUT THE TRUTH IS I'M SCARED TO DEATH! MY HANDS ARE SHAKING!

EVERYTHING HAS BEEN EXACTLY DUPLICATED!

IT'S UNBELIEVABLE!

LET'S SIT IN THE PILOT SEATS AND WAIT TO SEE WHAT HAPPENS...

THEY HAVEN'T CLOSED THE HATCH YET...

KIM! OUTSIDE!

WE'VE ALREADY MOVED! WE'RE IN A DIFFERENT PLACE!

INSTANT TRAVEL!

IT'S VERY STRANGE... THERE'S NO HORIZON, AS IF WE WERE ON AN ISLAND IN THE MIDDLE OF NOWHERE!

AND YET, ASIDE FROM THAT, THIS PLACE IS FAMILIAR. THIS SPIT OF SAND BETWEEN A RIVER AND THE SEA...

ALEXA! THIS IS THE PLACE WHERE LYNN VANISHED!

MAMA!

IS THIS ANOTHER HOLOGRAM, ALEXA? I DON'T THINK I CAN STAND IT!

I THINK THIS TIME ... IS DIFFERENT, KIM...

MAMAAAA!

MY DAUGHTER!

I FOUND YOU, MY LITTLE GIRL! I FOUND YOU!

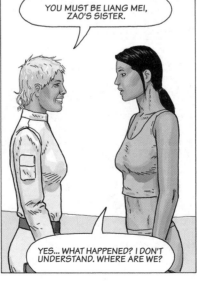

YOU MUST BE LIANG MEI, ZAO'S SISTER.

YES... WHAT HAPPENED? I DON'T UNDERSTAND. WHERE ARE WE?

IT'S A LONG STORY, MEI, AND HARD TO BELIEVE. YOU'RE GOING TO HAVE TO BE STRONG AND STAY CALM...

IT WAS WEIRD, MAMA! I WAS WITH MAI LAN, THEN ALL OF A SUDDEN I WAS IN A WHITE TUBE WITH THIS LADY NEXT TO ME. THERE WAS A DOOR AT THE BACK. WE TOOK IT, AND THEN I SAW YOU, MAMA!

THAT'S MORE OR LESS WHAT HAPPENED TO ME AS WELL. I WAS TALKING TO MY BROTHER AND SALIF WHILE WALKING TOWARDS OUR SHUTTLE, THEN THE NEXT MOMENT I WAS IN THAT WHITE TUNNEL ALONG WITH THIS LITTLE GIRL...

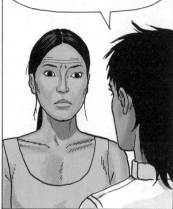

YOU WERE BOTH TAKEN BY A LIGHT BEAM PROJECTED FROM SPACE. AN UNEXPLAINED PHENOMENON. FOR LYNN, IT HAPPENED THREE MONTHS AGO. FOR YOU, MEI, THAT WAS OVER THREE YEARS AGO.

'I TOLD MEI EVERYTHING. EVERYTHING, POINT-BLANK. IT WAS THE ONLY WAY TO DO IT, AND SHE HAD THE RIGHT TO KNOW. IT WAS QUITE A SHOCK, OF COURSE, BUT SHE BORE IT WELL. SHE WAS A STRONG WOMAN, OBVIOUSLY USED TO KEEPING HER EMOTIONS UNDER CONTROL.'

'LYNN LISTENED INTENTLY, AND HER REACTION SUR-PRISED ME, AS USUAL WITH MY GIFTED DAUGHTER.'

YOU'VE BEEN LOOKING FOR ME FOR THREE MONTHS, MAMA!? WHOA! AND WE'RE ON A DIFFERENT PLANET? HOW DID I TRAVEL FROM ONE PLANET TO ANOTHER?

IT'S A MYSTERY, LYNN. WE DON'T UNDERSTAND IT EITHER...

SO WE'RE NOT OUT OF THE WOODS YET. HERE WE ARE IN THIS BIZARRE PLACE, AND YOU DON'T KNOW HOW TO LEAVE.

WE'LL USE THE SHUTTLE'S COPY, AS WE DID TO COME HERE IN THE FIRST PLACE.

WHAT SHUTTLE?

WHAT THE...?! WHEN DID IT DISAPPEAR?!

THERE WAS NO SHUTTLE WHEN WE ARRIVED.

I'M SO TIRED OF ALL THESE ABSURD EVENTS! I CAN'T STAND IT ANY MORE!

DOES YOUR HEAD HURT, MAMA?

17

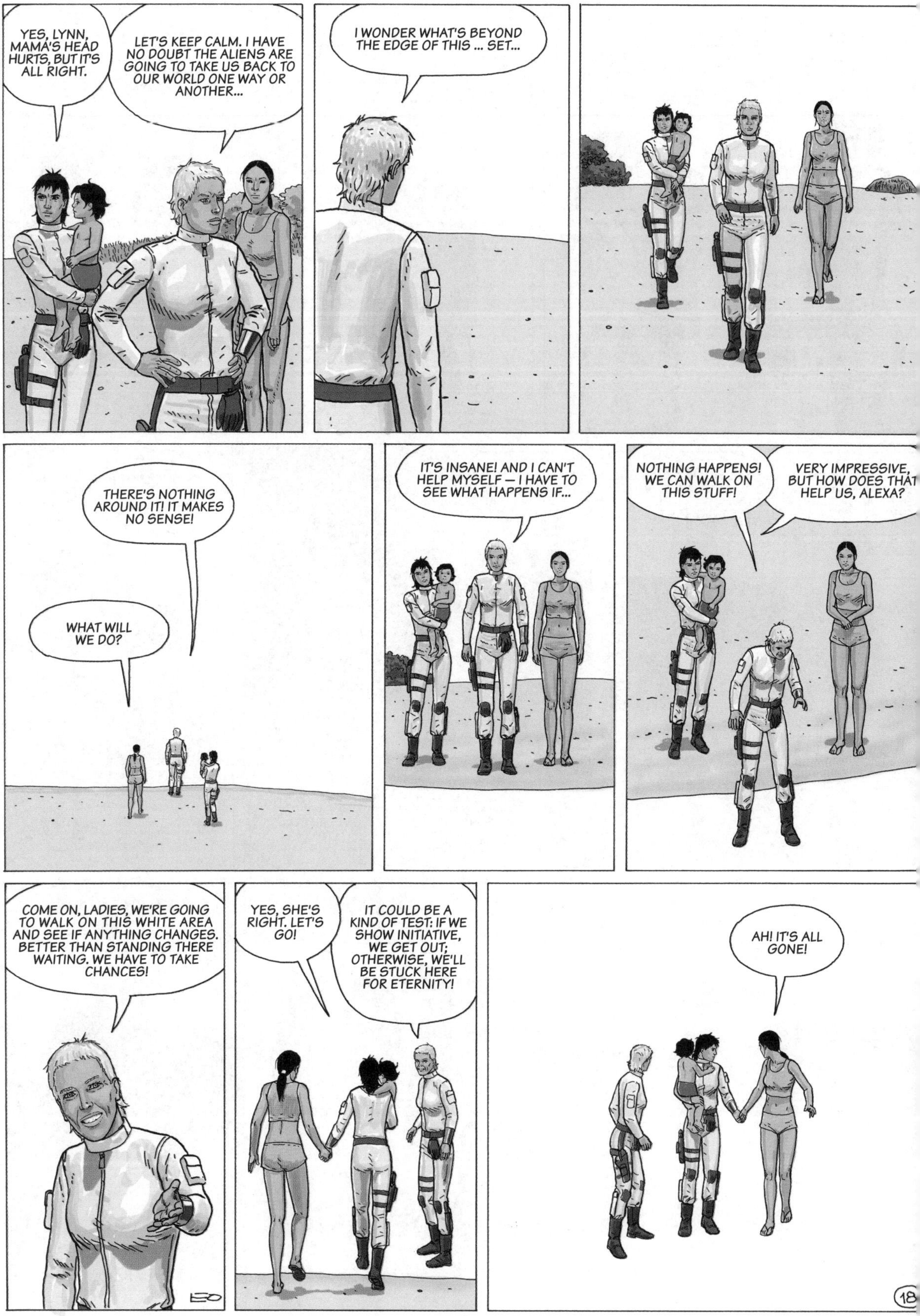
YES, LYNN, MAMA'S HEAD HURTS, BUT IT'S ALL RIGHT.
LET'S KEEP CALM. I HAVE NO DOUBT THE ALIENS ARE GOING TO TAKE US BACK TO OUR WORLD ONE WAY OR ANOTHER...
I WONDER WHAT'S BEYOND THE EDGE OF THIS ... SET...
THERE'S NOTHING AROUND IT! IT MAKES NO SENSE!
WHAT WILL WE DO?
IT'S INSANE! AND I CAN'T HELP MYSELF — I HAVE TO SEE WHAT HAPPENS IF...
NOTHING HAPPENS! WE CAN WALK ON THIS STUFF!
VERY IMPRESSIVE, BUT HOW DOES THAT HELP US, ALEXA?
COME ON, LADIES, WE'RE GOING TO WALK ON THIS WHITE AREA AND SEE IF ANYTHING CHANGES. BETTER THAN STANDING THERE WAITING. WE HAVE TO TAKE CHANCES!
YES, SHE'S RIGHT. LET'S GO!
IT COULD BE A KIND OF TEST: IF WE SHOW INITIATIVE, WE GET OUT; OTHERWISE, WE'LL BE STUCK HERE FOR ETERNITY!
AH! IT'S ALL GONE!
18

DAMMIT! SHALL WE TURN BACK TOWARDS...?

THE TUBE! IT'S SIMILAR TO THE ONE WE WERE IN BEFORE...

THERE! I SEE AN EXIT!

BEEP BEEP BEEP BEEP BEEP BEEP

WHAT IS THAT?

HUH?...

IS THE GHOST SHUTTLE BACK?

NO, NO SIGN OF THE SHUTTLE.

THE RADAR SHOWS SOMETHING APPROACHING. MAYBE AN ANIMAL...

COMING THIS WAY.

I DON'T SEE ANYTHING...

THERE!

I DON'T BELIEVE MY EYES!

MY GOD!

WHAT, ASHLEY?

19

25

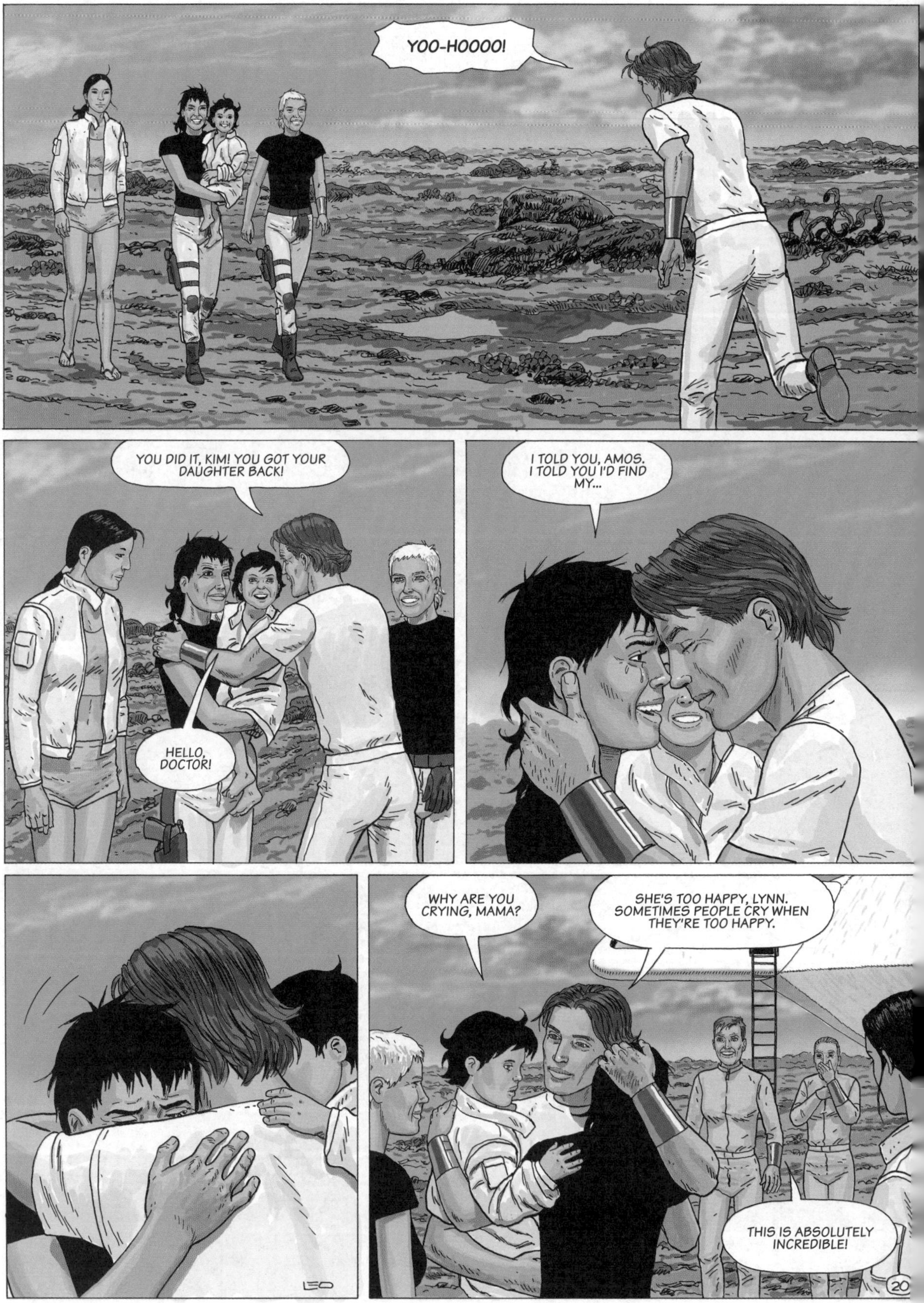
YOO-HOOOO!
YOU DID IT, KIM! YOU GOT YOUR DAUGHTER BACK!
HELLO, DOCTOR!
I TOLD YOU, AMOS. I TOLD YOU I'D FIND MY...
WHY ARE YOU CRYING, MAMA?
SHE'S TOO HAPPY, LYNN. SOMETIMES PEOPLE CRY WHEN THEY'RE TOO HAPPY.
THIS IS ABSOLUTELY INCREDIBLE!
LEO
20

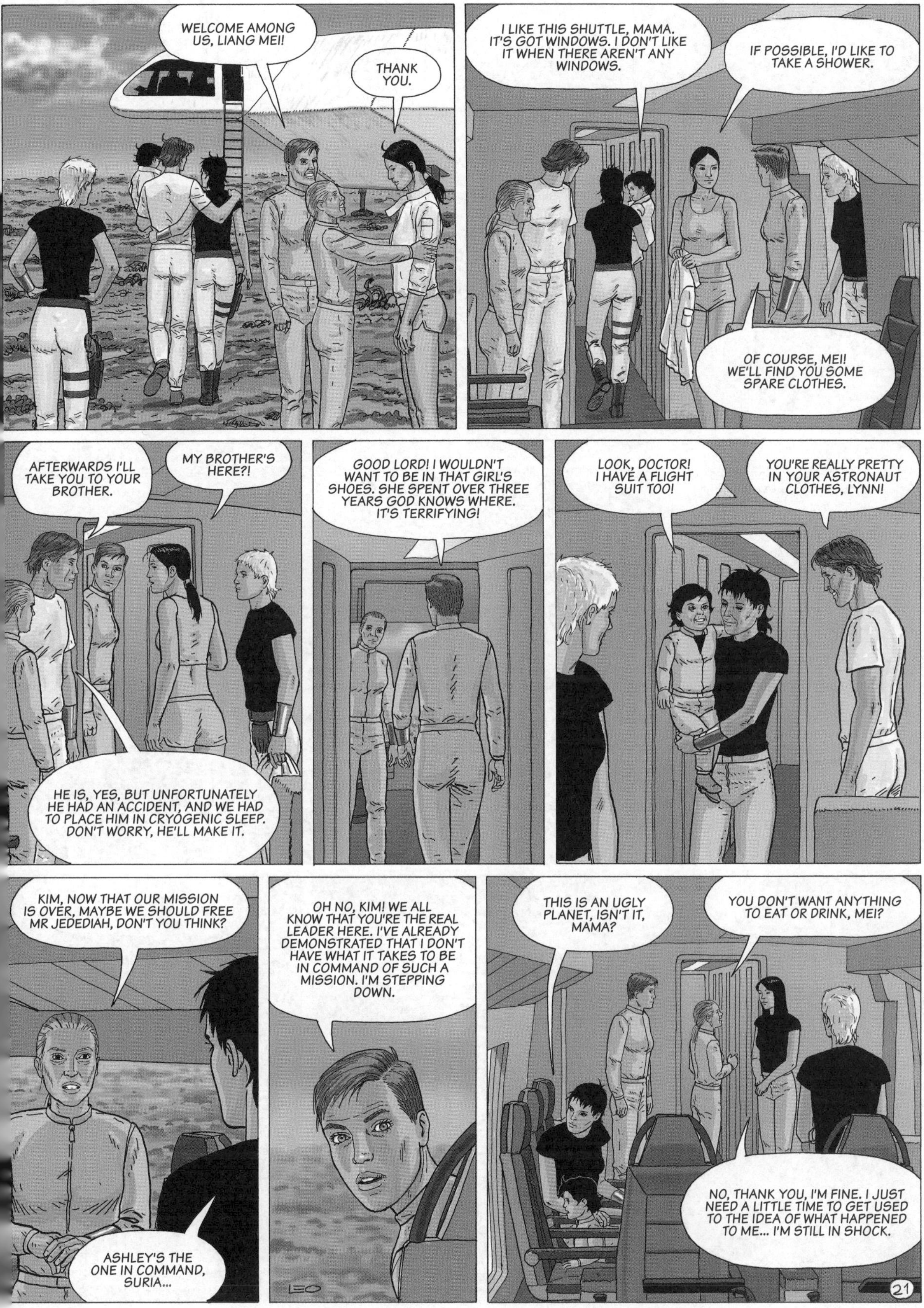

WELCOME AMONG US, LIANG MEI!
THANK YOU.
I LIKE THIS SHUTTLE, MAMA. IT'S GOT WINDOWS. I DON'T LIKE IT WHEN THERE AREN'T ANY WINDOWS.
IF POSSIBLE, I'D LIKE TO TAKE A SHOWER.
OF COURSE, MEI! WE'LL FIND YOU SOME SPARE CLOTHES.
AFTERWARDS I'LL TAKE YOU TO YOUR BROTHER.
MY BROTHER'S HERE?!
HE IS, YES, BUT UNFORTUNATELY HE HAD AN ACCIDENT, AND WE HAD TO PLACE HIM IN CRYOGENIC SLEEP. DON'T WORRY, HE'LL MAKE IT.
GOOD LORD! I WOULDN'T WANT TO BE IN THAT GIRL'S SHOES. SHE SPENT OVER THREE YEARS GOD KNOWS WHERE. IT'S TERRIFYING!
LOOK, DOCTOR! I HAVE A FLIGHT SUIT TOO!
YOU'RE REALLY PRETTY IN YOUR ASTRONAUT CLOTHES, LYNN!
KIM, NOW THAT OUR MISSION IS OVER, MAYBE WE SHOULD FREE MR JEDEDIAH, DON'T YOU THINK?
ASHLEY'S THE ONE IN COMMAND, SURIA...
OH NO, KIM! WE ALL KNOW THAT YOU'RE THE REAL LEADER HERE. I'VE ALREADY DEMONSTRATED THAT I DON'T HAVE WHAT IT TAKES TO BE IN COMMAND OF SUCH A MISSION. I'M STEPPING DOWN.
LEO
THIS IS AN UGLY PLANET, ISN'T IT, MAMA?
YOU DON'T WANT ANYTHING TO EAT OR DRINK, MEI?
NO, THANK YOU, I'M FINE. I JUST NEED A LITTLE TIME TO GET USED TO THE IDEA OF WHAT HAPPENED TO ME... I'M STILL IN SHOCK.
21

AND HERE'S OUR LOVABLE JEDEDIAH, FREE AND IN PERFECT HEALTH.

YOU'VE GOT YOUR DAUGHTER BACK, KIM KELLER, BUT YOU FAILED IN YOUR MISSION. YOU DIDN'T SPEAK TO THE ALIENS. YOU MESSED UP EVERYTHING WHEN YOU LOCKED ME UP! WHEN WE GET BACK TO BASE, I WILL MAKE SURE YOU'RE ARRESTED FOR ABUSING YOUR AUTHORITY.

YOUR CONFINEMENT WAS JUSTIFIED, JEDEDIAH THORNTON. YOUR BEHAVIOUR HAS BEEN A CONSTANT DANGER TO THIS MISSION. I WILL TESTIFY IN KIM KELLER'S FAVOUR.

BESIDES, IF KIM DIDN'T SPEAK TO THE ALIENS, IT'S BECAUSE THEY NEVER SHOWED UP. IT'S NOT HER FAULT!

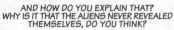

AND HOW DO YOU EXPLAIN THAT? WHY IS IT THAT THE ALIENS NEVER REVEALED THEMSELVES, DO YOU THINK?

NO WAY! DON'T TELL ME YOU ACTUALLY THINK IT'S BECAUSE YOU WEREN'T THERE?! BECAUSE THERE WERE ONLY WOMEN?! HOW CAN ANYONE BE SO OBTUSE, JEDEDIAH? SO RIGIDLY STUPID?!

YOUR INSULTS MEAN NOTHING TO ME, AMOS BLUM, BECAUSE I HAVE FAITH. I KNOW THAT I AM GUIDED BY OUR LORD, AND THAT HE LED US TO THIS FARAWAY WORLD TO MEET ALIENS!

SUCH IS HIS WILL... FOR THE HUMAN RACE TO JOIN WITH A MORE ADVANCED SPECIES SO THAT WE MAY SERVE HIM WITH EVEN GREATER STRENGTH!

BEEP BEEP BEEP BEEP BEEP

WHAT'S THAT...?

A SHIP'S APPROACHING!

THERE! OUTSIDE!

IT'S THAT SMALL ALIEN SHUTTLE!

LET ME WELCOME THEM! YOU PEOPLE STAY IN HERE!

22

NO! STAY INSIDE! YOU'RE GOING TO RUIN EVERYTHING AGAIN!

STOP SHOUTING, JEDEDIAH! YOU'RE THE ONE WHO'LL RUIN EVERYTHING!

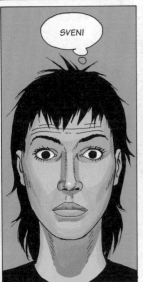

SVEN!

ALEXA, THAT'S SVEN! IT'S HIM I MET ON BETELGEUSE... HE'S LYNN'S FATHER!

WHAT?!

WELCOME! WE ARE HUMAN BEINGS FROM PLANET EARTH. I AM JEDEDIAH, THEIR LEADER, A MAN OF FAITH AND VIRTUE!

I AM VERY PLEASED TO M...

NO, DON'T PAY ATTENTION TO HER! SHE'S JUST AN UNDERLING. I, JEDEDIAH THORNTON, AM THE MAN IN CHARGE OF THIS MISSION!

KIM!

SVEN! I DIDN'T EXPECT TO SEE YOU AGAIN...

I NEVER EXPECTED TO SEE YOU AGAIN EITHER, KIM!

WHAT...?!

LEO

23

29

I'M DELIGHTED TO SEE LYNN ALIVE AND WELL!
SHE LOOKS LIKE YOU.
YOU...! YOU...! YOU KNOW EACH OTHER?!
I... I DON'T UNDERSTAND!... I DON'T...
YES, JEDEDIAH, I MET KIM ONCE BEFORE, A FEW YEARS AGO. AND IT IS TRUE THAT THERE ARE MANY THINGS YOU DON'T UNDERSTAND!
YOU DON'T UNDERSTAND, FOR EXAMPLE, THAT I'M THIS LITTLE GIRL'S FATHER. AN IMPROBABLE BIRTH, SINCE DIFFERENT SPECIES AREN'T SUPPOSED TO BE ABLE TO PROCREATE TOGETHER.
BUT KIM ISN'T A NORMAL HUMAN. SHE WENT THROUGH THE MUTATIONS CAUSED BY THE MANTRIS. BUT I DIGRESS; THE MAIN THING IS THAT I'M HERE TO SEE MY DAUGHTER — TO SEE LYNN.
IT'S NICE TO MEET YOU, LYNN. DO YOU KNOW THAT I'M YOUR FATHER?
YES, I KNOW. AND THAT'S WHY I HAVE MY MAGICAL EYES. THEY'RE LIKE YOURS.
YES, YOU GOT THEM FROM ME. BUT EVERYTHING ELSE YOU INHERITED FROM YOUR MOTHER, AND YOU'RE AS BEAUTIFUL AS SHE IS.
THAT'S TRUE; MAMA IS VERY BEAUTIFUL. THAT'S WHY UNCLE MARK AND THE DOCTOR ARE IN LOVE WITH HER. ARE YOU IN LOVE WITH MY MAMA TOO?
OH YES! I'M IN LOVE WITH YOUR MAMA TOO!
MAY I ASK YOU A QUESTION, SVEN? NOW THAT I'M BEGINNING TO RECOVER FROM THE SHOCK OF SEEING A HUMANOID ALIEN FOR THE FIRST TIME ... AND ONE WHO SPEAKS MY LANGUAGE, TOO!
GO AHEAD, ALEXA.
AS YOU'RE LYNN'S FATHER, IT OBVIOUSLY WASN'T YOU, YOUR PEOPLE, WHO TOOK HER OR OPERATED THE SPHERES. SO WHO DID? DO YOU KNOW WHO THEY ARE?
NO. NO ONE HAS EVER SEEN THEM.
LEO
24

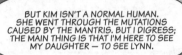

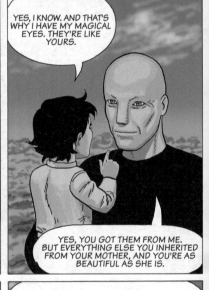

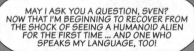

SO YOU'RE NOT THE ALIENS WHO CONTROLLED THE SPHERE! I KNEW IT! YOU'RE NOT THE SUPERIOR BEINGS I CAME HERE TO MEET!

YOU'RE NOTHING BUT A MINOR RACE, AND A SINFUL ONE AT THAT! YOU STOOPED SO LOW AS TO HAVE IMPURE RELATIONS WITH ONE OF OUR WOMEN! YOU'RE NOT A WORTHY SPECIES!

JEDEDIAH, YOU'RE A PATHETIC MAN! YOU'RE THE EMBODIMENT OF EVERYTHING THAT'S STILL TOXIC AND BACKWARD IN HUMANS.

MY PEOPLE ARE MUCH MORE ADVANCED SCIENTIFICALLY THAN YOUR OWN, AND WE'VE BEEN OBSERVING YOU EVER SINCE YOU ARRIVED ON ALDEBARAN. AT ONE POINT, OUR LEADERS DISCUSSED THE POSSIBILITY OF MAKING CONTACT WITH YOU, TO HELP YOU SPEED UP YOUR EVOLUTION BY SHARING SCIENTIFIC KNOWLEDGE WITH YOU...

BUT THEY ABANDONED THE IDEA. DO YOU KNOW WHY? BECAUSE OF TYPES LIKE YOU. MY PEOPLE BELIEVE THAT A SOCIETY THAT CONTAINS A SIGNIFICANT NUMBER OF INDIVIDUALS THAT THINK LIKE YOU IS AN UNDERDEVELOPED SOCIETY.

AND A POTENTIALLY DANGEROUS ONE, TOO. PEOPLE LIKE YOU USURP THE RIGHT TO HOLD THE TRUTH. THEIR HEADS ARE FILLED ONLY WITH ABSOLUTE CERTAINTIES, AND THEY FIGHT ALL WHO DO NOT SHARE THOSE CERTAINTIES.

PEOPLE LIKE YOU ARE A SENSELESS SOURCE OF UNNECESSARY TRAGEDY AND PAIN, JEDEDIAH THORNTON!

YOU'RE WRONG! I AM A PIOUS AND VIRTUOUS MAN WHO MERELY OBEYS GOD'S WILL! I HAVE FAITH, AND I KNOW THAT THE BEINGS BEHIND THAT SPHERE SHARE MY BELIEFS! I CAME HERE TO MEET THEM, NOT YOU!

DON'T BE RIDICULOUS! MY PEOPLE, AS WELL AS SEVERAL OTHERS FROM THIS GALAXY, HAVE VISITED THIS PLANET, AND HAVE KNOWN OF THIS SPHERE FOR CENTURIES. WE'VE STUDIED IT TO TRY AND UNDERSTAND WHAT WAS GOING ON HERE. AND OUR CONCLUSION IS THIS: THERE'S NO ONE BEHIND THE SPHERE.

25

IT'S A ROBOT. A VERY SOPHISTICATED ONE, BUT STILL JUST A MACHINE, TAKING ACTION SOLELY BY FOLLOWING A PROGRAM GIVEN TO IT HUNDREDS OF YEARS AGO. IT TAKES ITS ENERGY FROM ANY MATTER THAT TOUCHES ITS SURFACE. ITS MISSION IS TO CONDUCT GENETIC EXPERIMENTS ON THE FAUNA FROM THE PLANET YOU INTENDED TO COLONISE.

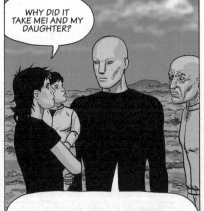

WHY DID IT TAKE MEI AND MY DAUGHTER?

TO STUDY THEM. THEY WERE UNKNOWN BEINGS, WHICH IT DETERMINED BY ANALYSING THE BLOOD SAMPLES TAKEN BY ITS SMALL FLYING ROBOTS. USING ITS ENERGY BEAM IT BROUGHT THEM TO THIS PLANET, ITS BASE, TO STUDY THEM.

HOWEVER, WHEN IT MAKES ITS USUAL HARVEST OF ANIMALS, THEIR FELLOW CREATURES DON'T REACT. OFTEN THEY DON'T EVEN NOTICE. BUT TAKING ADVANCED BEINGS SUCH AS YOU TRIGGERED A RESPONSE, AND THE SPHERE DIDN'T KNOW HOW TO PROCEED.

FORTUNATELY, IN YOUR CASE IT RETURNED THE SUBJECTS UNHARMED. THAT'S NOT THE USUAL WAY: IT'S PROGRAMMED TO DESTROY THEM AFTER ANALYSIS.

DO YOU SEE, JEDEDIAH? THAT SPHERE WAS BUILT BY A VERY ANCIENT, HIGHLY TECHNOLOGICALLY ADVANCED PEOPLE — BUT ONE THAT'S BEEN GONE FOR HUNDREDS AND HUNDREDS OF YEARS. AND NO ONE CAN TELL WHEN THEY'LL COME BACK, ASSUMING THEY EVER DO...

IF YOU'RE STILL BENT ON MEETING THEM, BE PREPARED TO WAIT A LONG, LONG TIME. AND IF YOU HOPE THAT THEY'LL SHARE THE SAME RETROGRADE OPINIONS AS YOU, WELL...

WHOOPS!

I THINK HIS BELIEFS MAY HAVE BEEN TOO SEVERELY SHAKEN...

I'LL TAKE CARE OF HIM!

BUT I'M CURIOUS TO HEAR WHAT YOU CAME HERE TO DO, SVEN. YOU AND YOUR... IS SHE YOUR PARTNER?

OH NO! HER NAME IS ELTVEN, AND SHE'S MY SUPERIOR. SHE HOLDS A VERY HIGH RANK IN OUR SPATIAL ORGANISATION, AND I CAME HERE WITH HER BECAUSE WE NEEDED TO TALK TO YOU, KIM.

TALK TO ME...

ABOUT WHAT?

ABOUT YOUR DAUGHTER, OF COURSE.

ELTVEN DOESN'T SPEAK YOUR LANGUAGE. SHE HAS TO USE A VOICE TRANSLATOR. UNFORTUNATELY, IT SPEAKS IN A COLD, IMPERSONAL MANNER. PLEASE UNDERSTAND THAT.

WHAT ABOUT MY DAUGHTER?

I'D LIKE TO TELL YOU IN PRIVATE. WOULD YOU MIND JOINING ME ABOARD MY SHIP?

YOU CAN SPEAK IN FRONT OF EVERYONE. I'M SICK OF SECRETS. I DON'T WANT TO KEEP ANYTHING FROM THE OTHERS ANY MORE.

NO, I CANNOT SPEAK IN FRONT OF THE OTHERS.

IT'S IMPORTANT, KIM.

YOUR DAUGHTER MEANS A LOT TO US. BEYOND THE FACT THAT SHE IS THE ONLY LIVING LINK BETWEEN OUR TWO PEOPLES, SHE ALSO HAS UNUSUAL ABILITIES.

WE WANT HER TO BE KEPT SAFE.

YOUR DAUGHTER INHERITED MORE THAN HER UNUSUAL PUPILS FROM HER FATHER. SHE ALSO INHERITED HIS METABOLISM... AS YOU DISCOVERED DURING THE AQUATIC PHASE LYNN WENT THROUGH IN HER FIRST YEARS.

YOUR DAUGHTER IS NOW IN THE TERRESTRIAL PHASE OF HER DEVELOPMENT, AND YOU CAN LIVE WITH HER AS IF SHE WERE 100 PER CENT HUMAN. BUT THIS PHASE WILL END IN A LITTLE OVER A YEAR, AND LYNN WILL ONCE AGAIN HAVE FINS AND GILLS.

27

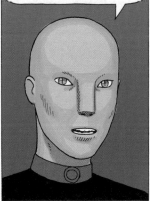

SHE WILL THEREFORE BE UNABLE TO BREATHE THE AIR AND WILL HAVE TO RETURN TO AN AQUATIC ENVIRONMENT. WHEN SHE WAS A TODDLER, YOU WERE ABLE TO IMPROVISE TO GET HER THROUGH THAT PHASE, BUT THIS TIME THAT WON'T BE POSSIBLE...

...BECAUSE THE AQUATIC STAGE WILL LAST UNTIL THE END OF PUBERTY — IN OTHER WORDS, 11 OR 12 YEARS.

IT'S A KEY STAGE IN HER PERSONALITY DEVELOPMENT. SHE MUST BE AROUND YOUTHS OF HER AGE, AND SHE MUST RECEIVE APPROPRIATE SCHOOLING, OF COURSE.

YOU UNDERSTAND THAT THE ONLY PLACE WHERE SHE CAN DO ALL THAT IS ON OUR WORLD. SHE MUST COME AND LIVE WITH US.

BUT WILL SHE BE ACCEPTED? SHE'S HALF HUMAN — SHE'S PHYSICALLY DIFFERENT!

NOT THAT MUCH. AND OUR PEOPLE ARE USED TO MEETING BEINGS FROM OTHER PLANETS. YOUR DAUGHTER WILL FEEL PERFECTLY AT EASE WITH US. I GUARANTEE IT!

AND ME? WILL I NOT BE ABLE TO SEE HER AGAIN? I'M HER MOTHER!

I HAVEN'T YET BEEN ABLE TO OBTAIN OUR GOVERNMENT'S AUTHORISATION FOR YOU TO ACCOMPANY YOUR DAUGHTER. OUR LAWS DON'T ALLOW IT. AND IT'S VERY COMPLICATED TO CHANGE THEM.

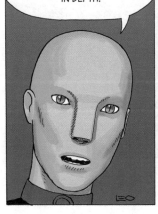

BUT I'M SURE IT WON'T BE TOO LONG BEFORE YOU'RE PERMITTED TO COME AND SEE YOUR DAUGHTER. AT THIS VERY MOMENT, OUR RELATIONSHIP WITH YOUR PEOPLE IS BEING DEBATED IN DEPTH.

YOU WERE EXPECTING THAT, WEREN'T YOU?

YES, OF COURSE. I KNEW IT WOULD COME SOONER OR LATER. I MUST ADMIT THAT IF MY DAUGHTER RETURNED TO HER AQUATIC FORM FOR SUCH AN EXTENDED TIME, I'D BE COMPLETELY AT A LOSS...

DO YOU HAVE TO LEAVE WITH HER RIGHT AWAY?

THOSE WERE INDEED MY ORDERS. BUT AFTER ALL YOUR EFFORTS TO FIND YOUR DAUGHTER, I COULD NEVER DO SUCH A THING TO YOU. I THINK I CAN ARRANGE FOR YOU TO KEEP HER FOR THE DURATION OF HER NON-AQUATIC PHASE.

28

...AND THEN SHE TOLD ME THAT IT WAS TOO EARLY TO DISCUSS IT FURTHER. THAT I MUST RETURN TO THE BASE — WITH LYNN — AND THAT THEY'D CONTACT ME WHEN THE TIME CAME.

MY GOD! THIS IS ALL SO EXTRA-ORDINARY! AND YOU, KIM... YOU'VE GOT A DAUGHTER WHOSE FATHER IS AN ALIEN, NO LESS!

IT MUST HAVE BEEN VERY HARD FOR YOU TO KEEP SUCH A SECRET FOR SO LONG, KIM!

I THINK THE WORST IS YET TO COME, SURIA. ONCE WORD GETS OUT, I'LL BE THE CENTRE OF ATTENTION: I'M THE FIRST PERSON TO MEET A HUMANOID ALIEN, AND I HAD A CHILD WITH HIM! CAN YOU IMAGINE THE UPROAR WHEN PEOPLE HEAR ABOUT IT?!

WE'RE GOING NOW, AND LEAVING LYNN WITH YOU. WE'LL CONTACT YOU SOON ON ANTARES 5. EXPECT GREAT CHANGES.

GREAT CHANGES...

IT WAS GREAT TO MEET YOU, LYNN. I HOPE YOU'RE HAPPY TO KNOW THAT I'M YOUR FATHER.

YES ... BUT IT'S GOOD THAT I DIDN'T GET YOUR NOSE. IT'S A VERY FUNNY NOSE. I LIKE MAMA'S BETTER.

I AGREE, LYNN. I FIND YOUR MAMA'S NOSE MUCH PRETTIER THAN MINE TOO!

I JUST MET ALIENS! I STILL CAN'T BELIEVE IT!

WE CAN START PREPARING FOR OUR RETURN TRIP.

YES! MISSION ACCOMPLISHED: WE'VE RECOVERED YOUR DAUGHTER AND ZAO'S SISTER. INCREDIBLE!

WHAT'S THAT...?

TWiiiiiNNN

29

35

JEDEDIAH! I'D FORGOTTEN ABOUT THAT GUY!

WHAT ARE YOU DOING, JEDEDIAH? WHERE ARE YOU GOING?

PERHAPS HE WANTS TO RETURN TO THE PLACE WHERE WE FOUND THE SPHERE.

YES, HE'S PROBABLY CONVINCED THE OTHER ALIENS ARE GOING TO APPEAR TO HIM!

AND THERE'S LITTLE POINT IN TRYING TO MAKE HIM SEE REASON. HE'S TOO STUBBORN.

I DON'T THINK HE'S TRYING TO GO ANYWHERE...

WHAT DO YOU MEAN, DOCTOR? SURELY YOU DON'T THINK HE'S...

NO!

SEVERAL DAYS LATER, BACK AT BASE CAMP...

36

THERE SHE IS!

MAI LAN!

LYNN!

YOU DID IT, KIM! YOU DID IT!

MEI!

I'M SO HAPPY TO SEE YOU, MEI!

EASY, SALIF, YOU'RE GOING TO CRUSH MY RIBS!

ZAO?

HE RECEIVED SURGERY AS SOON AS WE ARRIVED AT THE MOTHER SHIP. HE'S FINE. HE'LL MAKE A COMPLETE RECOVERY.

REUNIONS ARE BEAUTIFUL THINGS, AREN'T THEY, DOC?

THEY CERTAINLY ARE, PAD, VERY MOVING. ESPECIALLY LYNN AND MAI LAN'S.

JOHN NASH! HOW ARE YOU?

I'M VERY HAPPY TO SEE YOU SAFE AND SOUND. AND EVEN HAPPIER TO SEE THAT YOU GOT YOUR ADORABLE DAUGHTER BACK, KIM. IT'S INCREDIBLE!

I'M TO TAKE YOU TO YOUR NEW QUARTERS, AND THEN MR ELIJAH WOULD LIKE TO SEE YOU.

ALL RIGHT.

MARK, MAI LAN, WILL YOU COME WITH ME? I NEED TO TALK TO YOU.

AMOS, CAN YOU COME TOO?

31

WHERE WILL YOU STAY?

THEY PUT ME WITH THE SPACE CORPS OFFICERS, HERE AT THE AIRFIELD. BUT I'LL DROP BY LATER TO SAY HELLO.

THE WATER ROSE SO SUDDENLY THAT WE COULDN'T SAVE MUCH. A COMPLETE DISASTER!

BUT THE WORST OF IT HAPPENED HERE AT THE MINE. WE HAD FATALITIES — PEOPLE WHO WERE TRAPPED INSIDE WHEN THE WATER ARRIVED... WE HAD TO WRITE OFF ALL THE HEAVY EQUIPMENT. MR THORNTON HAS ALREADY OFFICIALLY ANNOUNCED THAT FORWARD ENTERPRISES IS GOING INTO BANKRUPTCY.

YOU'LL BE STAYING HERE, AT THE FORMER ACCOMMODATION OF THE MINE'S MANAGEMENT. I'LL COME BACK IN AN HOUR TO TAKE YOU TO MR THORNTON. IS THAT ALL RIGHT?

ABSOLUTELY, JOHN.

MAMA, I'M TIRED. I'D LIKE TO GO TO SLEEP.

OK, LET'S GO AND FIND THE BEDROOM IN OUR NEW HOUSE.

I SUPPOSE YOU WANT TO SPEAK TO MARK AND MAI LAN?

YES... WOULD YOU MIND...?

SO, LYNN, WOULD YOU LIKE ME TO TELL YOU A STORY BEFORE SLEEP, OR WOULD YOU RATHER LISTEN TO SOME MUSIC?

MUSIC. THOSE CHOIRS WE WERE LISTENING TO YESTERDAY.

YESTERDAY?!... AH, RIGHT...

ER... WE NEED TO CHAT...

NO NEED. I THINK I KNOW.

WHAT?

YOU BOTH LOOK LIKE KIDS WHO'VE DONE SOMETHING NAUGHTY...

BETTER TO MAKE THINGS EASIER FOR YOU BY ADMITTING THAT I, TOO, HAVE TO TELL YOU SOMETHING. DURING THIS OH-SO-STRESSFUL MISSION, I REALISED THAT I FELT A VERY STRONG ATTRACTION TOWARDS AMOS BLUM. I THINK I'VE HAD THIS FEELING FROM THE MOMENT I MET HIM.

A BIT LIKE YOU TWO, NO? I'VE ALWAYS FELT THAT YOU WERE ATTRACTED TO MAI LAN RIGHT FROM THE START, MARK. AND SHE TO YOU. I SUPPOSE THAT WHILE YOU WERE HERE ALONE THESE PAST FEW DAYS, SOMETHING STARTED BETWEEN YOU. AM I WRONG?

NO, YOU'RE NOT WRONG.

I THINK IF YOU PUT THOSE TWO FACTS TOGETHER, IT SHOWS THAT THERE WAS ALREADY A CRACK IN OUR RELATIONSHIP, MARK. WE WANTED... I, ESPECIALLY, WANTED TO RELIVE OUR EARLY LOVE STORY. BUT TIME HAS PASSED. OUR LIVES HAVE CHANGED; WE'VE MOVED ON AND TAKEN DIFFERENT PATHS. YOU SAW IT YOURSELF NOT LONG AGO, MARK.

YOU'RE VERY IMPORTANT TO ME AND YOU'RE SURELY MY BEST FRIEND. BUT NOW I'M IN LOVE WITH AMOS ... AND I THINK YOU'RE IN LOVE WITH MAI LAN.

WE'VE LIVED SOME VERY INTENSE MOMENTS, YOU AND I, AND THOSE MOMENTS WILL BE OURS FOR EVER.

I'LL ASK YOU TO LEAVE, NOW, OR THINGS WILL GET AWKWARD BETWEEN US... BESIDES, I'M SURE THE TWO OF YOU WANT TO BE ALONE.

YOU'RE NOT ANGRY WITH ME, KIM, ARE YOU? NOTHING'S GOING TO CHANGE BETWEEN US?

NO, MAI LAN, NOTHING'S GOING TO CHANGE BETWEEN US...

MY BROTHER WAS A SICK MAN. I CAN SEE THAT CLEARLY NOW. HIS MESSIANIC FAITH WAS A SYMPTOM I FAILED TO IDENTIFY. I EVEN LET MYSELF BE DRAGGED INTO HIS FANTASIES. HE WAS MY ELDER BROTHER, AND HE'D ALWAYS BEEN ABLE TO DRAW ME INTO HIS DREAMS AND HIS MADNESS.

I DON'T THINK HE WAS A SICK MAN. HE WAS A FANATIC. THERE'S A DIFFERENCE. FANATICISM ISN'T A DISEASE; IT'S AN ATTITUDE, A CHOICE. YOUR BROTHER DID US A LOT OF HARM. LIANG ZAO ALMOST DIED BECAUSE OF HIM.

I HOLD YOU RESPONSIBLE FOR ALL THAT. YOU WERE THE ONE WHO IMPOSED HIS PRESENCE ON OUR MISSION. JUST LIKE YOU WERE THE ONE WHO GAVE FREE REIN TO THE CULT THAT CAUSED SO MUCH SUFFERING AND HUMILIATION AMONG THE MEMBERS OF THE ANTARES PROJECT.

I UNDERSTAND YOUR BITTERNESS TOWARDS ME ... AND I THINK YOU'RE RIGHT, AT LEAST PARTIALLY. I WASN'T ABLE TO FORESEE WHERE MY BROTHER'S EXCESSES WOULD LEAD. I GAVE HIM FREE REIN, AS YOU PUT IT. BUT IF IT MAKES YOU FEEL ANY BETTER...

...I'M FINISHED. I LOST EVERYTHING. MY COMPANY, YES, BUT ABOVE ALL MY DREAM. MY DREAM OF BUILDING SOMETHING GREAT HERE. A NEW LAND, WHERE PEOPLE COULD HAVE LIVED IN HARMONY AND ABUNDANCE.

YOU'RE WRONG. SEEING YOU SUFFER DOESN'T MAKE ME FEEL BETTER AT ALL...

I UNDERESTIMATED YOU, MISS. YOU TRULY ARE AN EXTRAORDINARY PERSON. I SHOULD HAVE GIVEN YOU A POSITION COMMENSURATE WITH YOUR SKILLS. I DIDN'T MAKE USE OF THEM, OR OF...

BLEEP

SORRY, I MUST TAKE THIS. IT'S FROM THE ADMIRAL AND FLAGGED AS URGENT.

GO AHEAD, ADMIRAL.

ELIJAH, IS KIM KELLER WITH YOU?

YES, SHE'S HERE.

ARE YOU AWARE THAT THE ALIENS ENCOUNTERED BY THE MISSION TO ANTARES 4 INTEND TO MAKE CONTACT WITH HUMANITY?...

YES, I WAS TOLD.

WE THOUGHT THEY'D WANT TO SPEAK TO THE TOP LEADERS OF EARTH, DURING SOME WELL-ADVERTISED, LARGE-SCALE INTERNATIONAL MEETING...

...WELL, WE WERE WRONG! TURN ON YOUR SCREEN, ELIJAH, YOU WON'T BELIEVE YOUR EYES!

GOOD LORD!

NO, ELIJAH, YOU'RE NOT DREAMING. THE ALIENS ARE HERE, AND THEY WANT TO ESTABLISH CONTACT WITH HUMANS RIGHT HERE ON ANTARES, THROUGH US!

THEY ASKED TO MEET TWO OF THE MAIN LEADERS AMONG US. WE DECIDED THAT WOULD BE SURIA KHALEB TO REPRESENT THE UN, AND MYSELF, AS THE HIGHEST RANKING OFFICER OF THE SPACE CORPS HERE.

BUT THEY ALSO WANT TWO OTHER PEOPLE TO BE PRESENT: KIM KELLER AND — BRACE YOURSELF — ALEXA KOMAROVA! WE MENTIONED THAT MRS KOMAROVA DOESN'T HOLD A RANK AND THAT SHE WAS EVEN UNDER A TEMPORARILY SUSPENDED PRISON SENTENCE.

THEY SAID THEY KNEW BUT STILL INSISTED ON ALEXA KOMAROVA'S PRESENCE. THEREFORE I MUST ASK YOU TO SEND THOSE TWO UP TO OUR ORBIT AS QUICKLY AS POSSIBLE, ELIJAH.

IF MY BROTHER HAD LIVED, I DOUBT HE COULD'VE ENDURED WHAT'S HAPPENING NOW: THE FACT THAT WOMEN, WHOM HE CONSIDERED INFERIOR AND UNWORTHY, HAVE BEEN CHOSEN BY A MORE ADVANCED PEOPLE TO PARTICIPATE IN THIS FIRST CONTACT!

YES, FATE SPARED HIM THIS 'ABOMINATION'...

35

I CAN UNDERSTAND WHY THEY'D ASK FOR YOU, BUT ME? ARE YOU SURE YOU DON'T HAVE ANY IDEA? YOU SPOKE TO THAT ALIEN WOMAN FOR A LONG TIME...

I SWEAR I DON'T, ALEXA. TO BE HONEST, I DON'T SEE WHY I MUST BE MIXED UP IN IT ALL EITHER.

THIS IS NOTHING LESS THAN THE FIRST OFFICIAL ENCOUNTER WITH PEOPLE FROM ANOTHER WORLD IN ALL OF HUMANKIND'S HISTORY! WHAT WOULD A GIRL LIKE ME, BORN IN A TINY VILLAGE SUCH AS ARENA BLANCA IN A BACKWARD COLONY SUCH AS ALDEBARAN, HAVE TO DO WITH ANY OF THIS?

WELL, WE'LL KNOW SOON ENOUGH...

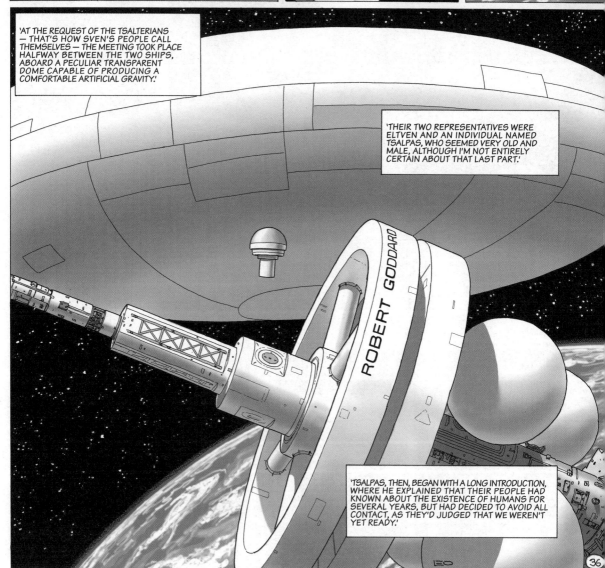

'AT THE REQUEST OF THE TSALTERIANS — THAT'S HOW SVEN'S PEOPLE CALL THEMSELVES — THE MEETING TOOK PLACE HALFWAY BETWEEN THE TWO SHIPS, ABOARD A PECULIAR TRANSPARENT DOME CAPABLE OF PRODUCING A COMFORTABLE ARTIFICIAL GRAVITY.'

'THEIR TWO REPRESENTATIVES WERE ELTVEN AND AN INDIVIDUAL NAMED TSALPAS, WHO SEEMED VERY OLD AND MALE, ALTHOUGH I'M NOT ENTIRELY CERTAIN ABOUT THAT LAST PART.'

ROBERT GODDARD

'TSALPAS, THEN, BEGAN WITH A LONG INTRODUCTION, WHERE HE EXPLAINED THAT THEIR PEOPLE HAD KNOWN ABOUT THE EXISTENCE OF HUMANS FOR SEVERAL YEARS, BUT HAD DECIDED TO AVOID ALL CONTACT, AS THEY'D JUDGED THAT WE WEREN'T YET READY.'

36

'ONLY RECENTLY HAVE THEY BEGUN RE-CONSIDERING THEIR POSITION. MOSTLY BECAUSE OF THE OBSERVATIONS SVEN MADE OF THE GROUP OF PEOPLE WHO TOOK THE MANTRIS'S CAPSULES.'

THAT SCIENTIST WAS SO FAVOURABLY IMPRESSED BY THOSE PARTICULAR HUMANS THAT HE MANAGED TO CONVINCE A MAJORITY OF OUR AUTHORITIES. SO, THE DECISION TO ESTABLISH CONTACT WITH YOUR PEOPLE WAS MADE.

BUT IT'S A VERY SMALL MAJORITY, AND THERE ARE MANY CONDITIONS.

COMMUNICATION WITH YOU HUMANS WILL HAPPEN VERY GRADUALLY. WE WILL NOT GO TO EARTH, WE WILL NOT MEET YOUR LEADERS. ALL CONTACT WILL TAKE PLACE ON THE PLANET YOU CALL ALDEBARAN, IN AN ISOLATED SPOT, WITH A VERY SMALL GROUP OF HUMANS.

BUT WHY? WE DON'T UNDERSTAND!

WE HAVE OUR REASONS. OUR ARRIVAL ON A HIGHLY POPULATED PLANET SUCH AS YOUR EARTH WOULD CAUSE AN IN-DESCRIBABLE UPHEAVAL, WHICH COULD HAVE DIRE CONSEQUENCES FOR YOUR ECONOMY AND YOUR SOCIAL STRUCTURE.

WE DON'T WANT GOVERNMENT-TO-GOVERNMENT RELATIONS FOR THIS FIRST CONTACT, EITHER. WE WOULD LIKE TO SUGGEST THAT TWO GROUPS OF SCIENTISTS, ONE FROM EACH SPECIES, COLLABORATE ON A RESEARCH PROJECT. SUCH A COLLABORATION WOULD BE THE FIRST STEP IN THE LONG PROCESS OF BRINGING OUR TWO PEOPLES TOGETHER.

WE PROPOSE THAT YOUR GROUP OF SCIENTISTS IS LED BY KIM KELLER AND THAT SHE DECIDES ON ITS MEMBERS.

37

43

WHY NOT GIVE US THE RIGHT TO CHOOSE THAT CONTACT GROUP OURSELVES, RATHER THAN IMPOSE YOUR CHOICE UPON US?!

WE'RE NOT IMPOSING ANYTHING. WE'RE MERELY ESTABLISHING CONDITIONS. YOU'RE FREE NOT TO ACCEPT THEM ... IN WHICH CASE THERE WILL BE NO CONTACT BETWEEN OUR PEOPLES, AT LEAST FOR THE MOMENT.

AND WHAT WOULD THE TWO SCIENTIFIC TEAMS WORK ON?

THEY WOULD HAVE TO CONTINUE RESEARCH THAT WE'D BARELY STARTED, IN AN ISOLATED CORNER OF ONE OF ALDEBARAN'S CONTINENTS. A CONTINENT YOU'VE HARDLY EVER VISITED SO FAR.

THE MISSION'S DETAILS WILL BE GIVEN TO KIM KELLER. IT'LL BE UP TO HER TO FORWARD THEM TO YOU LATER.

WHY ME? WHY CHOOSE ME TO LEAD THE TEAM FROM EARTH? I'M TOO YOUNG! THERE HAVE TO BE SCIENTISTS MUCH MORE CAPABLE AND EXPERIENCED THAN ME!

DON'T UNDERESTIMATE YOURSELF, KIM KELLER. THE SCIENTIFIC KNOWLEDGE YOU LACK CAN BE PROVIDED BY THE SPECIALISTS YOU CHOOSE. BUT WE WANT YOU AS LEADER BECAUSE WE KNOW YOUR OTHER QUALITIES...

THIS MISSION WILL ENTAIL SOME FIELDWORK, AND WILL REQUIRE PEOPLE WITH A CERTAIN TYPE OF EXPERIENCE AS WELL AS A *GOOD* AMOUNT OF COMMON SENSE. PEOPLE LIKE YOU.

38

THIS IS ALL VERY DISAPPOINTING! CONTACT BETWEEN OUR RACES WILL ACTUALLY BE LIMITED TO CONTACT BETWEEN VERY FEW INDIVIDUALS!

THERE WILL BE TWO MORE PERSONS INVOLVED.

WE PROPOSE THAT A REPRESENTATIVE OF YOUR PEOPLE BE SENT TO US. AN AMBASSADOR.

FOR THAT TASK, WE WANT ALEXA KOMAROVA — ALONG WITH HER FRIEND PROFESSOR DRISS SHEDIAC.

THIS IS UNACCEPTABLE! A PEOPLE MUST CHOOSE THEIR OWN REPRESENTATIVE! AND MRS KOMAROVA DOESN'T HAVE THE STATURE NEEDED FOR SUCH A POSITION! WHAT'S MORE, SHE'S A CRIMINAL! SHE'S SERVING A PRISON SENTENCE!

THE CHOICE OF ALEXA KOMAROVA IS ONE OF THE CONDITIONS FOR CONTACT BETWEEN US TO BE ESTABLISHED.

OF ALL THE HUMANS PRESENT HERE ON THIS PLANET, SHE IS THE OLDEST, MOST EXPERIENCED AND MOST LEVEL-HEADED. SHE'S ALSO THE VERY FIRST MEMBER OF THE MANTRIS GROUP. IT'S A DETERMINING FACTOR TO US.

AS FOR THE FACT THAT, ACCORDING TO YOUR CUSTOMS, SHE IS CONDEMNED TO BE LOCKED UP... WE SHARE NEITHER YOUR JUDGEMENT NOR YOUR METHODS. WE DON'T LOCK UP SOMEONE WHO'S MADE A MISTAKE. TO US, ALEXA KOMAROVA REMAINS A PERSON OF GREAT VALUE.

ER... WOULD WE HAVE TO LIVE ON YOUR PLANET FOR LONG?

A FAIRLY LONG TIME, YES. BUT THIS STAY WILL BE ADVANTAGEOUS TO YOU. IT WILL ALLOW US TO MAKE A FEW CORRECTIONS IN THE MUTATION THE MANTRIS CAUSED IN YOUR BODY. WE NOTICED THAT YOU SUFFERED FROM A FEW IMBALANCES.

IMBALANCES?

YES. WE NOTICED THAT THE EFFECTS OF THE MANTRIS'S CAPSULE ON THE HUMAN ORGANISM SOMETIMES REQUIRED A FEW ADJUSTMENTS IN ORDER TO IMPROVE YOUR PSYCHO-LOGICAL COMFORT.

39

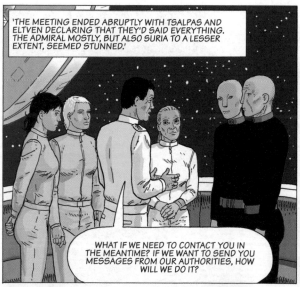

'THE MEETING ENDED ABRUPTLY WITH TSALPAS AND ELTVEN DECLARING THAT THEY'D SAID EVERYTHING. THE ADMIRAL MOSTLY, BUT ALSO SURIA TO A LESSER EXTENT, SEEMED STUNNED.'

WHAT IF WE NEED TO CONTACT YOU IN THE MEANTIME? IF WE WANT TO SEND YOU MESSAGES FROM OUR AUTHORITIES, HOW WILL WE DO IT?

WE DO NOT WISH TO STAY IN CONTACT WITH YOUR AUTHORITIES. ANY COMMUNICATION WILL HAVE TO GO THROUGH ONE PERSON ONLY: KIM KELLER.

I WILL INSTALL A DEVICE ON HER WRIST COMMUNICATOR TO LET HER CALL US.

'THE FIRST MEETING BETWEEN HUMANS AND A PEOPLE FROM ANOTHER PLANET HAD UNFOLDED IN A COMPLETELY UNEXPECTED MANNER. THE ADMIRAL WAS GOING TO FIND IT DIFFICULT TO MAKE HIS REPORT TO EARTH.'

CLACK

THIS IS ALL COMPLETELY INSANE!

STAY, PLEASE. WE'D LIKE YOU TO ACCOMPANY US TO OUR SHIP, SO WE CAN GIVE YOU INFORMATION ON THE RESEARCH MISSION.

THIS ARRANGEMENT, KIM, WILL ALLOW YOU TO STAY WITH YOUR DAUGHTER FOR ANOTHER YEAR, AS LONG AS IT'S IN A REMOTE CORNER OF ALDEBARAN.

SOMEWHERE WHERE YOUR DAUGHTER AND YOU WON'T BE UNDER SIEGE FROM THE MEDIA AND POPULAR CURIOSITY. LYNN'S WELFARE IS IMPORTANT TO US.

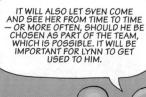

IT WILL ALSO LET SVEN COME AND SEE HER FROM TIME TO TIME — OR MORE OFTEN, SHOULD HE BE CHOSEN AS PART OF THE TEAM, WHICH IS POSSIBLE. IT WILL BE IMPORTANT FOR LYNN TO GET USED TO HIM.

WAIT A MINUTE — AT NO POINT HAVE YOU ASKED EITHER KIM OR ME WHETHER WE AGREE WITH YOUR PLANS FOR US...

TO WHAT PURPOSE?

40

THIS PROCESS OF BRINGING OUR SPECIES TOGETHER RESTS ON THESE PROPOSALS, WHICH ARE THE RESULT OF EXTREMELY HOT DEBATE BETWEEN OUR DECISION MAKERS. IF YOU WERE TO REFUSE THEM, IT WOULD CANCEL EVERYTHING. ARE YOU READY TO ASSUME SUCH A RESPONSIBILITY?

'HIS ARGUMENT CARRIED A HINT OF IM-PERIOUSNESS THAT I FOUND DISTURBING. HE WAS RIGHT, THOUGH: THE STAKES WERE SO ENORMOUS THAT NEITHER ALEXA NOR I HAD A SAY IN THE MATTER.'

I'LL LEAVE YOU WITH ELTVEN.

WE'VE BEEN VISITING ALDEBARAN FOR A VERY LONG TIME — A LITTLE LESS SINCE YOUR OWN ARRIVAL THERE. A FEW YEARS AGO, ONE OF OUR SHIPS DETECTED A WEAK SOURCE OF RADIATIONS IN A PLACE LOCATED ON THE UNINHABITED CONTINENT YOU CALL WESTLAND.

WHAT PIQUED THE CREW'S CURIOSITY WAS THAT THERE WAS AN EXTREMELY COMPLEX PATTERN TO THOSE RADIATIONS. LOOKING FOR THE SOURCE, THEY DISCOVERED THIS...

'ELTVEN'S MOTION CAUSED A VERY REALISTIC HOLOGRAPHIC IMAGE TO APPEAR.'

A LARGE CUBE FLOATING IN THE AIR, WITH NO TRACE OF AN OPENING.

I'LL LET YOU WATCH ONE OF THE SCENES OF THAT DISCOVERY. THE SPOKEN EXCHANGES WERE TRANSLATED SPECIFICALLY FOR YOU.

41

47

I'VE GOT SOMETHING HERE! THIS AREA SHOWS A STRONG ALTERATION OF THE DELTA RESONANCE!

IT'S RIGHT HERE...

THIS PART OF THE CUBE SEEMS IMMATERIAL!

ALMOST BY ACCIDENT, THESE SCIENTISTS DISCOVERED THAT WITH A CERTAIN FREQUENCY OF DELTA WAVES, IT WAS POSSIBLE TO MAKE THE CUBE WALL PERMEABLE; OR, MORE SIMPLY, ONE COULD OPEN A DOOR ALLOWING ACCESS TO THE INTERIOR.

AND WHAT WAS INSIDE?

NOTHING. IT'S AN EMPTY SPACE. BUT SOME KINDS OF DOORS OPEN ON TO PASSAGES...

LEADING WHERE?

WE DON'T KNOW. NOT YET. WE INTERRUPTED OUR RESEARCH BECAUSE OF THE PRESENCE OF HUMANS ON ALDEBARAN. THIS WILL BE OUR CHANCE TO RESUME OUR INVESTIGATIONS — JOINTLY, THIS TIME.

42

WE'LL GIVE YOU MORE DETAILS LATER SO THAT YOU CAN PUT YOUR GROUP TOGETHER, KIM.

FOR NOW, A SMALL SHUTTLE WILL TAKE YOU TO YOUR SHIP.

AS FOR YOU, ALEXA, YOU MUST STAY HERE WITH US, AS WE'RE GOING TO LEAVE WITHOUT FURTHER DELAY.

WHAT, IMMEDIATELY?

YES. IS SOMETHING PREVENTING YOU? SPARE CLOTHES AND TOILETRIES WILL BE PROVIDED.

FROM HERE WE'LL HEAD FOR ALDEBARAN, WHERE WE'LL PICK UP YOUR COMPANION PROFESSOR SHEDIAC. YOU'LL HAVE THE OPPORTUNITY TO CONTACT HIM DURING THE TRIP TO WARN HIM.

...

I'LL LEAVE YOU ALONE FOR A WHILE SO YOU CAN SAY GOODBYE.

WHAT'S HAPPENING TO US IS SO EXTRAORDINARY, SO... SO ASTOUNDING! AND IT'S ALL TAKEN PLACE SO QUICKLY!

I'M ABOUT TO LEAVE FOR THE HOME PLANET OF A MORE ADVANCED CIVILISATION! RIGHT NOW! WITH DRISS, TOO! THIS IS INCREDIBLE!

I WON'T SEE YOU AGAIN FOR WHO KNOWS HOW LONG!

OUR ALIEN FRIENDS CERTAINLY DON'T HAVE ANY QUALMS ABOUT TURNING OUR LIVES UPSIDE DOWN AT THE DROP OF A HAT.

BUT I'M NOT COMPLAINING, QUITE THE CONTRARY! AND I HAVE A FEELING THAT YOU'RE HAPPY WITH THESE NEW POSSIBILITIES OPENING UP BEFORE YOU. TO WORK WITH A GROUP OF ALIEN SCIENTISTS AND STUDY THAT FASCINATING CUBE!

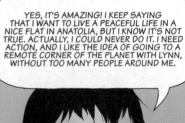

YES, IT'S AMAZING! I KEEP SAYING THAT I WANT TO LIVE A PEACEFUL LIFE IN A NICE FLAT IN ANATOLIA, BUT I KNOW IT'S NOT TRUE. ACTUALLY, I COULD NEVER DO IT. I NEED ACTION, AND I LIKE THE IDEA OF GOING TO A REMOTE CORNER OF THE PLANET WITH LYNN, WITHOUT TOO MANY PEOPLE AROUND ME.

43

BUT THERE'S MORE TO IT, ALEXA. THEY'VE GIVEN ME THAT OVERWHELMING JOB OF BEING THE ONLY ONE WHO CAN SPEAK TO THEIR LEADERS. EVERYTHING MUST GO THROUGH ME!

I'M ONLY 26! MOST WOMEN MY AGE JUST GO HOME AT NIGHT TO BE WITH THEIR HUSBANDS AND CHILDREN, TO MAKE DINNER, WATCH TV AND GO TO SLEEP...

BUT HERE I AM, BILLIONS OF MILES FROM MY HOME WORLD, AND THEY MAKE ME ONE OF THE KEY ELEMENTS OF HUMANKIND'S FIRST ENCOUNTER WITH PEOPLE FROM A DIFFERENT PLANET!

IT'S ME, KIM KELLER, BORN AND BROUGHT UP IN THE TINY VILLAGE OF ARENA BLANCA, THAT THE LEADERS OF A MORE ADVANCED SPECIES HAVE CHOSEN TO ASSUME THIS VITAL STRATEGIC FUNCTION!

I'M SCARED, ALEXA! I'M SCARED I WON'T BE GOOD ENOUGH, SCARED I'LL CRACK, DISAPPOINT EVERYONE, JEOPARDISE THE GOOD RESULTS OF THIS INITIAL CONTACT.

AT THE SAME TIME, I FEEL A BIT EUPHORIC. MOSTLY BECAUSE OF YOU: THEY'VE RECOGNISED YOUR WORTH, ALEXA! AND DRISS'S! THAT'S FANTASTIC! I CAN'T THINK OF TWO PEOPLE BETTER SUITED TO THE JOB THEY'VE GIVEN YOU.

TRUST THEM, THEN. IF THEY CHOSE YOU TOO, IT'S BECAUSE THEY SAW IN YOU THE IDEAL PERSON FOR THE JOB.

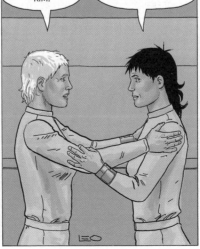

OH, I'M GOING TO MISS YOU, KIM!

I'M GOING TO MISS YOU TOO, ALEXA!

I REMEMBER THE DAY I SAW YOU FOR THE FIRST TIME. YOU WERE JUST A NAIVE KID, BUT I IMMEDIATELY FELT THAT THERE WAS SOMETHING SPECIAL ABOUT YOU. I WAS RIGHT.

44

AND I REMEMBER THE MOMENT I SAW YOU FOR THE FIRST TIME, WHEN YOU WERE A PRISONER OF THAT HORRIBLE FATHER LOOMIS!... HOW THINGS HAVE CHANGED SINCE THEN!

THAT'S TRUE!

IT'S TIME TO GO, KIM. WE'LL MEET AGAIN SOON.

I'LL TAKE YOU TO YOUR CABIN, ALEXA.

HANG IN THERE, KIM! AND DON'T WORRY, YOU'RE MORE THAN CAPABLE OF SHOULDERING THE RESPONSIBILITY THEY'VE GIVEN YOU.

'BEFORE HEADING DOWN TO THE SURFACE, I HAD TO TELL THE AUTHORITIES ON BOARD THE MOTHER SHIP WHAT HAD HAPPENED ON THE TSALTERIAN VESSEL. I COULD FEEL THEM PROBING ME, PERHAPS BECAUSE THEY WERE AFRAID THAT THE ENORMOUSLY IMPORTANT ROLE I'D HAD THRUST UPON ME MIGHT GO TO MY HEAD. I DID MY BEST TO PUT THEIR MINDS AT EASE.'

'TEN DAYS HAVE GONE BY. WE'RE SPENDING OUR LAST WEEK ON ANTARES 5 BEFORE THE ANTARES PROJECT SHIP RELOCATES TO THE NEW DESTINATION CHOSEN BY THE COLONISTS: ALDEBARAN, RATHER THAN A RETURN TO EARTH.'

'I'D DECIDED TO GATHER MY FRIENDS FOR A LITTLE PARTY BEFORE WE MUST RETURN TO THE SHIP'S CRAMPED ENVIRONMENT. I'M ALSO TRYING TO DELAY THE MOMENT WHERE I WILL BE LEFT ALONE WITH MY THOUGHTS.'

'MY LIFE IS ABOUT TO BE COMPLETELY TURNED UPSIDE DOWN YET AGAIN. SINCE MY TEENAGE YEARS, FATE HAS THROWN ME THIS WAY AND THAT, FROM DISASTERS TO BIZARRE MISSIONS, CHANGING PLANETS LIKE OTHERS CHANGE NEIGHBOURHOODS...'

45

'...IS THAT A LIFE? IS THAT WHAT I REALLY WANT? I ALSO HAVE MORE INTIMATE DOUBTS: WHEN I LEFT EARTH — ONLY FIVE MONTHS AGO — I WAS VERY HAPPY TO BE BACK WITH MARK. I WAS VERY MUCH IN LOVE WITH HIM. NOW I'M WITH AMOS BLUM, AND I'M SURE I'VE MADE THE RIGHT CHOICE.'

'AM I REALLY SURE, THOUGH? ONLY TIME WILL TELL, BUT I WISH I DIDN'T HAVE DOUBTS ABOUT IT. I WISH I WERE A LESS COMPLICATED PERSON.'

'I'LL HAVE TO RECRUIT A TEAM FOR THE MISSION TO ALDEBARAN. WHO AMONG THOSE PRESENT TONIGHT SHOULD I CHOOSE TO JOIN ME? AND WILL THEY ACCEPT THE INVITATION?'

'BUT MY BIGGEST WORRY, OF COURSE, IS ABOUT LYNN'S FUTURE. I'M GOING TO HAVE TO LET HER GO FAR AWAY FROM ME, TO ANOTHER PLANET! AND FOR A LONG TIME! HOW WILL SHE HANDLE THAT?'

ARE YOU ALL RIGHT? YOU SEEM TENSE, PREOCCUPIED. YOU BARELY SAID A WORD ALL EVENING.

TENSE, ME? NO... I'M FINE.

BE STRONG, KIM. BE STRONG!

END OF THE

ANTARES
CYCLE

SCRIPT, ARTWORK, COLOURS LEO
FEBRUARY 2015

(46)

FIRST CYCLE: ALDEBARAN

The first colonists arrived on Aldebaran in 2079. They were to be the first wave of a large influx of pioneers, coming from an overcrowded Earth to live on this apparently very hospitable new world. But an unexpected problem put a stop to the process: The second ship, with thousands of people onboard, disappeared mysteriously in mid-flight. On Earth, scientists were forced to admit that they hadn't quite mastered the incredibly complex phenomenon that allowed interstellar flights to overcome the speed-of-light barrier. So, all such travel was halted until the theoretical gaps could be filled and going to the stars could be done in complete safety. At the time, no one could have predicted that this interruption of flights would last a whole century. During that time, the first colonists on Aldebaran remained isolated on a wild planet and had to struggle to ensure their survival. As might be expected, they made mistakes, went to some unfortunate extremes… and the society they built reflected those: a military dictatorship mixed with an authoritarian church. The story of the Aldebaran cycle covers five years in the life of young Kim Keller, who lives in a small coastal village. She's only 13 at the beginning, and finds herself—quite against her will—drawn into a tragic series of events that will force her to grow up quickly so as not to be broken.

1 - The Catastrophe
Incl. The Blonde

2 - The Group
Incl. The Photo

3 - The Creature
Incl. The Betelgeuse Planet

SECOND CYCLE: BETELGEUSE

In 2184, a few years after interstellar flights resumed, mankind launched a second colonisation attempt, this time of a planet around the Betelgeuse star. The first ship, with over 3,000 people onboard, arrived without incident and remained in orbit while a team of technicians went down to the surface to prepare for the colonists' arrival. Soon afterwards, all communication with Earth mysteriously ceased. It took six years for Earth finally to send a rescue mission to Betelgeuse in order to find out what had happened—a small mission, with a reduced crew of only three: two astronauts and young Kim, now 24, who had just finished her biology studies on Earth. Once more, she would be swept into a series of events, often tragic and extraordinary, that would eventually change her life forever. After the six months she would spend on Betelgeuse, world of green canyons, she would never be the same person again.

1 - The Survivors
Incl. The Expedition

2 - The Caves

3 - The Other

	EARTH	ALDEBARAN-4	BETELGEUSE-6	ANTARES-5
Diameter	7,926 miles	8,157 miles	7,365 miles	7,954 miles
Surface gravity	1	1.2	0.89	1.001
Length of year	365 days	369 days	355 days	371 days
Length of day	23 hours 56 minutes	24 hours 36 minutes	23 hours 45 minutes	23 hours 41 minutes
Percentage sea/land	70/30	91/09	11/89	78/22
Relief: Max. height	29,029 feet (Everest)	15,682 feet (Saterjee)	31,972 feet (Van Gogh)	12,283 feet
Max. depth	37,795 feet	87,598 feet	17,585 feet	50,220 feet
Number of satellites	1	2	None	5

Clarifications concerning the naming of the planet

The names of extra-solar planets are derived by using the name of the star they orbit followed by a number indicating the planet's position in order of distance from said star. Thus, planet Aldebaran-4 is the fourth planet of the star Aldebaran. Aldebaran-4 being the only habitable planet of the system, common usage has led to dropping the number 4 to call it simply Aldebaran, thus confusing the name of the star and that of the planet.

It would be easy to imagine that the same thing would happen with Antares and that said planet would be a satellite of the star Antares. And yet, such is not the case: Antares is a red giant star with a diameter 500 times bigger than our Sun. It has no habitable worlds. The target planet for Project Antares, in fact, orbits a different star named GJ 1211 (GJ = Gliese-Jahreiss Catalog) and should itself be named GJ 1211-5—a drab name that was not at all to the taste of the project leaders. It so happens that this star, when seen from Earth, is just in front of Antares and is even masked by the red giant's much higher luminosity. To direct a telescope at GJ 1211, therefore, it is necessary to point it first at scarlet Antares, and then, using filters, seek the small, yellow dot of GJ 1211. This is how, quite naturally, it was decided to call planet GJ 1211-5 "Antares." A usurped name, yes, but so much more elegant!

ANTARES

The star Antares,
in the constellation Scorpius

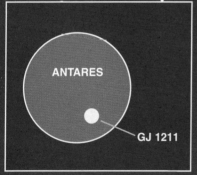

ANTARES

GJ 1211

The stars Antares and GJ 1211
as seen from Earth

One of the first photographs of the planet "Antares."
In the bottom left is the star Antares. On certain nights,
it bathes the surface of the planet in a rather
strong reddish glow.